200 christmas recipes

200 christmas recipes

hamlyn **all color**

An Hachette UK Company
www.hachette.co.uk

First published in Great Britain in 2010 by Hamlyn,
a division of Octopus Publishing Group Ltd,
Endeavour House
189 Shaftesbury Avenue
London
WC2H 8JY
www.octopusbooksusa.com

Distributed in the U.S. and Canada by Octopus Books USA:
c/o Hachette Book Group
237 Park Avenue
New York, NY 10017

Some of the recipes in this book have previously appeared in other
books published by Hamlyn.

ISBN: 978-0-600-62165-2

Printed and bound in China

1 2 3 4 5 6 7 8 9 10

Standard level spoon measurements are used in all recipes
1 tablespoon = one 15 ml spoon
1 teaspoon = one 5 ml spoon

Ovens should be preheated to the specified temperature—if
using a fan assisted oven, follow the manufacturer's instructions
for adjusting the time and the temperature.

Fresh herbs should be used unless otherwise stated.

Large eggs should be used unless otherwise stated.

The Food and Drug Administration advises that eggs should not
be consumed raw. This book contains some dishes made with raw
or lightly cooked eggs. It is prudent for vulnerable people, such
as pregnant and nursing mothers, invalids, the elderly, babies, and
young children to avoid uncooked or lightly cooked dishes made
with eggs. Once prepared, these dishes should be kept refrigerated
and used promptly.

This book also includes dishes made with nuts and nut derivatives.
It is advisable for those with known allergic reactions to nuts and
nut derivatives and those who may be potentially vulnerable to
these allergies, such as pregnant and nursing mothers, invalids,
the elderly, babies, and children, to avoid dishes made with nuts
and nut oils. It is also prudent to check the labels of pre-prepared
ingredients for nut derivatives.

contents

introduction

introduction

Sharing fine food with friends and family is at the heart of Christmas and, although it can be hard work, preparing the festive offerings yourself is part of the fun. Cooking is a great way to channel all that pre-Christmas anticipation and get the whole family involved. Many families have their own traditions and it is festive rituals, such as taking turns to stir the Christmas pudding mixture while making a wish, that form the fondest memories.

festive fare

For many people, Roast Turkey (see page 18) is the centerpiece of the main festive meal, followed by Traditional Christmas Pudding (see page 80). Other favorites include Roasted Goose with Spiced Apples (see page 36) and Roasted Duckling with Clementines (see page 42). If you don't eat meat, there are special centerpiece recipes such as Honey & Citrus Roasted Salmon (see page 38) or Feta and Roasted Vegetable Tart (see page 44).

For other celebration meals over the festive period, you'll want something other than turkey and Christmas pudding. For example, you could greet your guests with Champagne Strawberry Cup (see page 100), then serve them a homemade Chicken Liver Pâté (see page 74), followed by Beef Wellington (see page 40) and Bombe Noël (see page 86) to finish. The "Christmas Fare" chapter is packed with ideas for festive entertaining.

seasonal baking

Seasonal ingredients, such as mincemeat, nuts, cranberries, dried fruits, marzipan, and festive spices, including cinnamon, nutmeg, ginger, and cloves, make Christmas baking special. Rich Mince Pies (see page 134) are a must and there are plenty of other festive goodies to make. Baking is a great way of involving children in the festive preparations. Even very little children can help use cookie cutters to cut out star shapes, trees, and snowmen to make edible decorations for the Christmas tree (see pages 152 and 168), and afterward they will enjoy hanging up the decorated cookies with ribbon.

Cakes for Christmas come in all guises nowadays, from the fruit-packed Rich

Christmas Cake (see page 106) to novelty cakes to delight the children, such as the chocolate-crammed Santa's Bag (see page 108). If you would like a fruit Christmas cake, try to make it 1–3 months before Christmas. Store it in an airtight container and drizzle occasionally with a little brandy or sherry. You have the choice of leaving the cake uniced or covering it with marzipan and a white royal icing. Other festive cakes include the marzipan-rich Pistachio Nut Stollen (see page 122), the deliciously chocolaty Bûche de Noël (see page 114), and the nut-packed Panforte Di Siena (see page 128).

making edible gifts

Homemade preserves, cookies, and sweets make great Christmas gifts and you'll find plenty of inspiration in the "Edible Gifts" chapter. Creating attractive packaging is part of the fun. Look for pretty gift boxes and line them with coordinating tissue paper to

prevent the cookies or sweets from getting damaged. Alternatively, buy cellophane bags and secure them with invisible tape and festive ribbons and bows. If necessary, add a tag or label with storage instructions and an expiration date.

For homemade preserves, you'll need to prepare the jars thoroughly. Sterilizing the jars is a crucial stage of making your own chutneys, pickles, jams, and marmalades because the jars need to be spotlessly clean so the preserve will keep. Wash the jars in the dishwasher, or alternatively wash them in hot soapy water, rinse, and then dry them on the lowest setting in the oven for 15 minutes. Add the preserve to the still warm, dry jars, then press a disk of wax paper, waxed side down, onto the surface of the preserve while it is still hot. Let cool, then add a cellophane cover and secure with a rubber band or add a sterilized screw-topped lid (this is essential in the case of chutney to stop the vinegar from evaporating).

When the jars are filled and sealed, finish them with pretty seasonal jar covers and labels, available from good kitchenware stores. Label the jars with the name of the preserve, an expiration date, and any recommended serving instructions.

madeira cake

Madeira cake is a good base for decorated novelty cakes. The recipe given on page 10 is required for the Christmas Stocking (see page 120), Smiling Snowman (see page 126), and Christmas Trees (see page 140). The

quantities given below make a 12 x 9 x 2 inch baking pan cake or two 1-quart ovenproof bowl cakes.

1 cup (2 sticks) **unsalted butter**, softened
1¼ cups **superfine sugar**
4 **eggs**
2 tablespoons **milk**
1 teaspoon **baking powder** (for baking pan cake only)
2⅓ cups **self-rising flour**
2 teaspoons **vanilla extract**

Cream the butter and sugar together in a large bowl until light and fluffy. Beat the eggs and milk together in a small bowl with a fork. If using, mix the baking powder with the flour.

Beat alternate spoonfuls of the egg mixture and the flour mixture into the creamed mixture until everything has been incorporated and the cake mixture is smooth. Beat in the vanilla extract. Spoon the cake mixture into a greased and lined 30 x 23 x

12 x 9 x 2 inch baking pan or into two 1-quart ovenproof bowls.

Bake in a preheated oven at 325°F for 30–35 minutes for the baking pan and about 1 hour for the ovenproof bowls, until well risen and golden brown and a skewer inserted into the center of the cake comes out cleanly. Let stand for 10 minutes, then loosen with a round-bladed knife, turn out on to a wire rack, and let cool completely.

royal icing

Royal icing is the traditional icing used to cover celebration cakes. Depending on the consistency, it may be used for flat icing, peaked icing, or for piping on as decoration. This recipe makes 1 lb icing.

Glycerin, available from baking suppliers, is often used in royal icing to help soften the icing but should be used sparingly. Royal icing contains raw egg, which should not be eaten by children, pregnant women, the elderly, or those recovering from serious illness, unless it is pasteurized. Look out for pasteurized eggs in the supermarket, but if these are unavailable, then make up powdered egg white instead (sold in containers with other baking ingredients).

2 **egg whites**
¼ teaspoon **lemon juice**
4 cups **confectioners' sugar**, sieved
1 teaspoon **glycerin**

Place the egg whites and lemon juice in a clean bowl. Using a clean wooden spoon, stir to break up the egg whites. Add confectioners' sugar to form the consistency of light cream. Continue mixing while adding small quantities of confectioners' sugar until it is all used up, then stir in the glycerin until well blended. Cover with damp plastic wrap, seal well to exclude all air, then let stand before using so air bubbles can rise to the surface and burst. Stir thoroughly, to disperse any air bubbles, then apply using a palette knife.

ready-to-use fondant

Also known as rolled fondant icing, ready-to-use fondant is available in white and a range of colors from baking suppliers. You can also color white ready-to-use fondant by kneading in paste coloring, available from specialty cookshops. Roll out the fondant, then cut shapes using a sharp knife or cookie cutters.

Ready-to-use fondant can also be used as an overall smooth cake covering instead of

royal icing. To cover a cake in ready-to-use fondant, first spread the top and sides of your cake with smooth apricot jam or butter frosting. Knead the frosting on a surface lightly dusted with confectioners' sugar or cornstarch to soften it slightly, then roll it out. When the fondant is almost the same size as the top and sides of the cake, lift it over a rolling pin, then drape it over the cake. Working quickly, smooth the fondant in place over the top of the cake and down to the board, with your fingertips dusted with confectioners' sugar or cornstarch. When the fondant is in place, trim the excess from the bottom of the cake.

smooth apricot jam

Smooth apricot jelly or economy jelly doesn't contain fruit pieces so can be used straight from the jar for sticking marzipan and decorative icing directly onto cakes and cookies. If the jam has a very set texture, warm it briefly in the microwave before using. Alternatively, warm fruity apricot jam in a saucepan with a little boiled water and then strain it before use.

cutters

Plastic and metal cutters are useful for making shapes from ready-to-use fondant, cookie, and pastry dough and even cooled melted chocolate. Cutters come in a huge range of sizes and shapes. Ordinary round cutters have a myriad of uses. Gingerbread people are always popular shapes for cookies and you can also buy special Christmas cutters, including Santa, star, bell, Christmas tree, angel, snowman, holly leaf, ivy leaf, and reindeer shapes. You can even get three-dimensional cutters (see Winter Wonderland, page 156).

Wash cutters after use with a small bottle brush and dry metal ones in the bottom of a cooling oven to avoid rusting. When using small cutters, dip them in a little confectioners' sugar or cornstarch before use to prevent sticking. To release cutout shapes, press them out of the cutter using a fingertip or the rounded end of a small brush.

the turkey

A roasted turkey and all the trimmings is often the focus of the main Christmas meal. The turkey is not difficult to cook, but when there is so much else going on in the kitchen on Christmas morning, it's easy for the cook to become harassed.

Some forward planning will ensure smooth progress on the day. First work out the size of turkey you need for the number of people you are catering for, allowing for approximately 1 lb turkey weight per person. If it's to be a large turkey, check beforehand that your oven and roasting pan are big enough to take it.

There's a bewildering variety of turkeys available right before Christmas. Personal preference, availability, and budget will influence where you buy it and whether you choose fresh or frozen, whole or jointed, self-basted or prestuffed, organic, or conventionally reared. Any of these options will taste delicious if cooked correctly. Whatever kind of turkey, it should be at room temperature before it goes

in the oven and the cooking time should be based on its stuffed weight (see opposite).

fresh turkey

Fresh turkeys are available in supermarkets and butchers a week or so before Christmas, but it's best to order in advance to ensure you get the size you want.

If you're cooking for a small number or have only a small oven, consider buying a turkey joint instead of a whole turkey. A turkey crown is a whole turkey without the legs and wings, which gives you a joint of white breast meat on the bone. It's a popular choice because it is easy to carve and there's less wastage. Another option is a boned and rolled breast joint, which may come in netting to help it keep its shape. Remove the netting just before carving.

Remove the turkey from the refrigerator before you go to bed on Christmas Eve so that it comes to room temperature and will heat up as soon as you put it in the oven. Once you have taken the turkey out, you can fill the refrigerator with all the drinks that need to be chilled for Christmas Day.

frozen turkey

If you're using a frozen turkey, allow plenty of time for the bird to defrost slowly and completely before you come to cook it. Depending on the size of your bird, transfer it from the freezer to the refrigerator 2–6 days in advance of Christmas Eve and let it defrost gradually, allowing 8–12 hours defrosting time per 2 lb turkey.

Once the turkey is defrosted and there are no ice crystals remaining, remove all the packaging and take out the giblets. Store these separately until required for giblet stock (see page 14). Place the defrosted bird in a deep dish near the bottom of the refrigerator to prevent uncooked turkey juices dripping onto anything else. Then, as with a fresh bird, take the defrosted turkey out of the refrigerator at the last possible moment on Christmas Eve to let it come to room temperature before cooking.

TURKEY COOKING GUIDE

To calculate the cooking time at 375°F, allow 20 minutes per 2 lb, plus 70 minutes for birds under 8½ lb, or plus 90 minutes for birds weighing 8½ lb or more. These times apply whether you are cooking a whole stuffed bird or any turkey joint.

Turkey weight	Number of servings	Total cooking time
4½ lb	4–5	1 hour 50 minutes
5½ lb	5–6	2 hours
6½ lb	6–7	2 hours 10 minutes
7½ lb	7–8	2 hours 20 minutes
8½ lb	8–9	2 hours 50 minutes
10 lb	9–10	3 hours
11 lb	10–11	3 hours 10 minutes
12 lb	11–12	3 hours 20 minutes
13 lb	12–13	3 hours 30 minutes
14 lb	13–14	3 hours 40 minutes
15½ lb	14–15	3 hours 50 minutes
16½ lb	15–16	4 hours

cooking turkey to perfection

Make your chosen stuffing (see pages 22 and 24), then pack it loosely into the neck of the turkey—loosely because tightly packed stuffing would prevent heat from penetrating the center of the turkey. Similarly, don't stuff the body cavity of a whole bird because this may prevent it from cooking through completely. If you like, place an onion, fresh herbs or slices of lemon or orange in the body cavity, to give the meat additional flavors.

This book describes how to cook a perfect Roasted Turkey (see page 18) and Stuffed Turkey Breast Joint (see page 20). It is important to weigh the stuffed turkey to calculate the cooking time (see page 13) in a preheated oven, 375°F.

For tender meat, rub the bird all over with softened butter before cooking or cover the breast and legs with slices of bacon. Cover loosely with aluminium foil before cooking, then, during cooking baste with the cooking juices from time to time. Forty minutes before the end of cooking, remove the foil (discard the bacon if using), baste the turkey, and return to the oven, uncovered, to let the skin become crisp and brown.

is it cooked?

Check that a turkey (or other bird) is cooked by inserting a skewer into the thickest part of the thigh. The juices should run clear. If pink, cook for an additional 15 minutes and test again. Transfer the bird to a large dish, cover with clean foil, and let rest for 15–20 minutes. This resting time allows muscle fibers to relax

and become more tender, making the turkey easier to carve. Don't worry—its size means your roasted turkey will not go cold quickly.

carving the bird

Using a sharp knife, cut the skin between legs and breast. Bend each leg outward, cut through the joint, and remove the whole leg—it should fall away easily. Remove the wings in the same way. Now make a horizontal cut at the bottom of the breast as far as the bone, then cut downward to produce even slices of breast meat. Lastly, holding each drumstick in turn, slice the dark meat off the legs.

giblet stock

Giblet stock is the perfect base for gravy. Discard the liver (which can be bitter) and place the giblets of a turkey or other bird in a saucepan with 1 small quartered onion and

5 cups cold water. Bring to a boil, reduce the heat, cover, and simmer for 1 hour. Strain the stock into a pitcher.

leftover turkey

Cooked turkey can be kept in the refrigerator in aluminium foil or plastic wrap for up to 3 days. You can also freeze cooked turkey slices. Freezing in stock or gravy helps keep the meat moist. For ideas on how to use up the turkey after Christmas Day, turn to the "Leftover Turkey Ideas" chapter for inspiration. From Rigatoni with Turkey & Pesto (page 218) to Turkey Curry (page 228) and Country Turkey Pie (see page 232), you should find some appealing recipes to tempt the family.

boning a whole turkey

A boned turkey makes a wonderful casing for stuffing, a joint of meat, or another bird. A boned cavity and breast (see Steps 1–7) can be stuffed and reformed so it looks like a conventional bird when cooked. Continue boning the rest of the bird (Steps 8–9) to make a classic ballotine or galantine. A proper boning knife will make the task easy.

1 Cut off the ends of the legs and wings at the first joints.

2 Lift back the neck skin and cut out the wishbone and any surrounding fat.

3 Place the bird breast side down on the board and cut along the backbone, working from the tail to the neck end.

4 Holding the knife blade angled toward the carcass, scrape away the flesh from the rib cage, working down one side of the bird to the wing.

5 Ease the knife between the ball-and-socket joint and sever from the rib cage, while keeping it attached to the skin.

6 Continue easing away the flesh from the bone, using small scraping cuts, until you reach the leg joint, then sever the ball-and-socket joint in the same way as you dealt with the wing. Continue in this way until you have reached the ridge of the breastbone. Then turn the bird around and repeat Steps 1–6 on the other side.

7 Pull gently to separate the breastbone from the skin. There is no flesh here, so be careful not to tear the skin along the breastbone ridge or the bird will split open during cooking.

8 Lay the bird flat on the board, skin side down. Hold the outside of a wing bone and scrape away the flesh. Work top to bottom, severing tendons as you go. Pull out the wing bone. Repeat on the other wing. Push the skin and flesh of the wings back inside the carcass to make a neater parcel for stuffing.

9 Hold the inside of the leg bone and scrape away the flesh with a pencil-sharpening action. Sever tendons as you go, then release the bone when you get to the bottom of the leg. Repeat with the other leg.

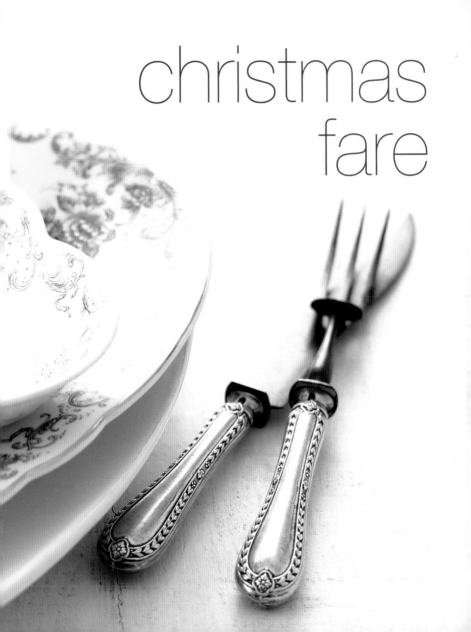

christmas fare

roasted turkey

Serves **10**, with leftovers
Preparation time **30 minutes**
Cooking time **3 hours**
  15 minutes–3 hours
  40 minutes, according
  to weight

1 quantity **Pecan Stuffing**
  (see page 22) or **Cranberry
  & Orange Stuffing** (see
  page 24)
11–13 lb **oven-ready turkey**,
  giblets removed and cavity
  wiped clean
1 small **onion**, halved
3 tablespoons **butter**,
  softened
2 tablespoons **vegetable oil**
3 **thyme sprigs**, chopped
salt and **black pepper**

Pack your chosen stuffing loosely into the neck of the bird and secure the neck flap with 2 crossed skewers. Place the onion in the body cavity and season the cavity with salt and black pepper. Tie the turkey legs together with twine at the top of the drumsticks.

Weigh the stuffed turkey to calculate the cooking time (see page 13), then place the bird in a large roasting pan. Rub all over with softened butter and season the outside of the turkey. Add the vegetable oil to the pan.

Cover the prepared turkey loosely with aluminium foil and roast in a preheated oven at 375°F for the required cooking time, basting from time to time. Remove the foil for the last 40 minutes of cooking to brown the bird and scatter over the chopped thyme. Check the turkey is cooked (see page 14).

Transfer the turkey to a large dish, cover with clean foil, and let rest for 15–20 minutes before carving. Meanwhile, pour off the fat from the roasting pan and use the juices to make gravy (see page 26).

Arrange the turkey on a warmed serving platter and serve with all the traditional accompaniments, such as Bacon & Chipolata Rolls (see page 26), Bread Sauce (see page 28), Brandied Cranberry Sauce (see page 30), and an assortment of vegetables.

stuffed turkey breast joint

Serves **7–8**

Preparation time **30 minutes**

Cooking time **3 hours**, or
according to weight

7½ lb **skin-on boned breast
joint**

8 tablespoons (1 stick) **butter**,
softened

1 **bay leaf**

2 tablespoons **vegetable oil**

salt and **black pepper**

Stuffing

1 tablespoon **vegetable oil**

½ large **onion**, finely chopped

1 **celery rib**, finely chopped

1 cup **mixed dried fruit**, finely
chopped

3 cups **fresh breadcrumbs**

1 cup finely chopped **mixed
shelled nuts**

½ medium **cooking apple**,
peeled, cored, and grated

1 tablespoon chopped
parsley

½ tablespoon chopped **thyme**

1 **egg**, beaten

Heat the oil for the stuffing in a pan, add the onion and
celery, and fry over a gentle heat, stirring frequently, for
about 10 minutes, until softened. Turn into a bowl, add
the remaining stuffing ingredients with salt and black
pepper to taste and mix well together. Set aside.

Ease your fingers between the turkey skin and the
breast meat. Push in the softened butter to cover the
breast completely. Place the turkey skin side down,
season with salt and black pepper, then spread with the
stuffing. Bring the turkey up and around the stuffing
to enclose it, making as neat and compact a shape as
possible, and secure with twine. Tuck a bay leaf under
the string.

Weigh the stuffed turkey to calculate the cooking time
(see page 13), add the vegetable oil to the roasting
pan, then place the turkey breast side up in the roasting
pan. Cover loosely with aluminium foil and roast in a
preheated oven at 375°F for the calculated cooking
time or until the juices run clear when the thickest part
is pierced with a skewer (see page 14). Remove the foil
for the last 40 minutes of cooking to brown the bird.

Lift the turkey out of the pan, cover tightly with foil, and
rest in a warm place for 15–20 minutes before serving.
Meanwhile, pour off the fat from the roasting pan and
use the juices to make gravy (see page 26). Place the
turkey on a warmed serving platter to serve.

pecan stuffing

Makes **enough for a 13 lb turkey**
Preparation time **5 minutes**
Cooking time **15 minutes**, plus turkey cooking time

heart and **liver** from a 13 lb **turkey**
1 cup **fresh bread crumbs**
⅓ cup finely chopped **shelled pecan nuts**
1 **egg**, hard-cooked and chopped
pinch of grated **nutmeg**
pinch of **ground mace**
1 tablespoon chopped **thyme**
1 tablespoon chopped **parsley**
pinch of **celery salt**
3 tablespoons **butter**
⅔ cup finely chopped **mushrooms**
1 small **onion**, chopped
2 tablespoons **dry sherry**
salt and **black pepper**

Put the heart and liver in a saucepan and cover with water. Bring to a boil and simmer for 10 minutes. Chop the meat finely and set aside to cool.

Place the chopped meat in a bowl and stir in the bread crumbs, nuts, egg, spices, herbs, and celery salt.

Melt the butter in a saucepan, add the mushrooms and onion, and cook over moderate heat, stirring frequently, for about 5 minutes, until softened. Stir into the meat mixture, add the sherry, and season to taste.

Pack the stuffing loosely into the neck of the turkey (see page 18) or shape into small balls and place in the tin around the turkey for the last 30 minutes of the turkey's cooking time.

For sweet potato & sausage-meat stuffing, melt 2 tablespoons butter in a skillet and fry 1 chopped onion and 2 chopped celery stalks until softened. Tip into a bowl and let cool, then stir in 2½ cups peeled and grated sweet potato, 1 lb pork sausage-meat, the grated zest of 1 lemon, and 1 cup chopped fresh herbs (such as parsley, oregano, sage, thyme). Mix well and finish cooking as above.

cranberry & orange stuffing

Makes **enough for a 13 lb turkey**
Preparation time **10 minutes**
Cooking time **13–16 minutes**, plus turkey cooking time

⅓ cup **sugar**
⅔ cup **water**
grated zest and juice of **1 orange**
2½ cups fresh or frozen **cranberries**, defrosted if frozen
2 cups mixed **long-grain** and **wild rice**
6 tablespoons **butter**
1 large **onion**, finely chopped
2 tablespoons chopped **parsley**
1 tablespoon chopped **thyme**
pinch of **ground cloves**
pinch of grated **nutmeg**
salt and **black pepper**

Put the sugar and water into a saucepan and stir over low heat until the sugar is dissolved. Bring to a boil and boil for 2–3 minutes. Add the orange zest and juice and the cranberries and stir with a wooden spoon, being careful not to crush the fruit. Simmer for 5 minutes until the sauce is translucent. Set aside.

Meanwhile cook the rice in a large pan of boiling salted water for 10–12 minutes, until just tender. Drain, rinse under cold water, and drain again.

Melt the butter in a saucepan and fry the onion over a moderate heat for 3–4 minutes, stirring once or twice. Remove from the heat.

Stir the rice, herbs, spices, and cranberry and orange mixture into the onions. Season with salt and black pepper and set aside to cool before packing loosely into the neck of the turkey (see page 18). Alternatively, cook in the oven for the last 30 minutes of the turkey's cooking time, either separately in an ovenproof dish or shaped into small balls and placed in the pan around the turkey.

For blueberry & orange stuffing, omit the cranberries and instead add 1⅔ cups blueberries to the dissolved sugar with the orange zest and juice, then continue with the recipe as above. Defrost first if using frozen blueberries.

bacon & chipolata rolls

Makes **16**
Preparation time **5 minutes**
Cooking time **16–20 minutes**

16 zestless **fatty bacon slices**
16 **pork chipolata sausages**

Stretch out the slices of streaky bacon using the back of a knife, then wind a slice along the length of each sausage.

Cook under a medium broiler for about 8–10 minutes on each side. Serve at least 2 per person alongside the Christmas roast.

For wine gravy, to serve with the turkey and trimmings, first make a stock from the giblets (see page 14) and set aside. While the cooked turkey is resting, spoon out all but 2 tablespoons of the fat from the roasting pan. Stir in 2 tablespoons all-purpose flour and cook gently on the stove top, stirring, for 1–2 minutes until golden. Add ⅔ cup full-bodied red wine, 2 cups hot giblet stock, a few drops of gravy browning, 2 tablespoons red-currant jelly, and salt and black pepper. Simmer, stirring, for 5 minutes, then serve.

For thin gravy, follow the recipe above but pour off *all* the fat from the roasting pan, leaving behind the sediment and pan juices. Set over high heat and pour in 3¾ cups hot giblet stock. Boil until reduced by about one-third. Reduce the heat to moderate, whisk in the finely grated zest and juice of 2 oranges, 4 tablespoons port or sherry, 2 tablespoons cranberry sauce or jelly, and salt and black pepper. Simmer, stirring, for a few minutes, then serve.

bread sauce

Serves **8**

Preparation time **10 minutes**, plus infusing

Cooking time **15–20 minutes**

1 small **onion**

3 whole **cloves**, plus extra to garnish (optional)

1 **bay leaf**, plus 1 to garnish (optional)

a few **parsley sprigs**

2 cups **milk**

1½ cups **fresh white bread crumbs**

3 tablespoons **butter**

⅔ cup **light cream**

grated **nutmeg**

salt and **black pepper**

Stud the onion with the cloves and place it in a saucepan with the bay leaf, parsley, and milk. Cover and bring slowly to a boil to let the milk better absorb the flavors. Remove the pan from the heat and let stand to infuse for 30 minutes.

Strain into a clean pan, discarding the onion and herbs. Stir in the bread crumbs and butter and cook over a very low heat, stirring occasionally, for 15 minutes. Stir in the cream and add nutmeg and salt and black pepper to taste. Garnish with a bay leaf and 2 or 3 cloves, if liked, and a final grating of nutmeg.

For reduced-fat bread sauce, follow the recipe above but omit the light cream and instead stir in ⅓ cup fat-free sour cream mixed with ⅓ cup whipping cream before adding the nutmeg and seasoning.

brandied cranberry sauce

Serves **6**
Preparation time **5 minutes**
Cooking time **5–10 minutes**

1¼ cups fresh or frozen
  cranberries, defrosted if
  frozen
⅔ cup **water**
2 tablespoons **packed light
  brown sugar**
pared zest of 1 **orange**
2 tablespoons **brandy**

Mix the cranberries, water, light brown sugar, orange zest and brandy together in a saucepan.

Cover the pan and cook over a low heat, stirring, for 5–10 minutes, until the cranberries burst.

For cranberry & orchard fruit sauce, finely chop 1–2 apples or pears and place in a saucepan with the cranberries, water, light brown sugar, grated orange zest, and brandy. Cook as above until the cranberries burst.

roasted beef sirloin

Serves **6–8**

Preparation time **15 minutes**, plus marinating

Cooking time **1 hour–1 hour 40 minutes**

3–4½ lb **boneless beef sirloin**

3 tablespoons **olive oil**

1 tablespoon **lemon juice**

1 large **onion**, thinly sliced

2 large **thyme sprigs** or **rosemary sprigs**

salt and **black pepper**

Dry the meat well. Rub it all over with the oil and drizzle over the lemon juice. Place half the onion slices and 1 thyme sprig in a dish, put the beef on top, and cover with the remaining onions and thyme sprig. Season with salt and black pepper. Cover and leave the beef in a cool place to marinate for at least 3 hours.

Discard the onions. Place the beef on a rack over a roasting pan to catch the meat juices. Put into the top of a preheated oven at 425°F. For rare beef, allow 15 minutes per 1 lb plus 15 minutes. For medium-done beef, allow 20 minutes per 1 lb plus 20 minutes. After 1 hour of cooking, reduce the temperature to 375°F. Baste occasionally with the pan juices.

Remove the beef from the roasting pan and let it rest on the rack, covered with a tent of aluminium foil. Carve the beef into slices and serve with Red Wine Sauce (see below) and roast potatoes and vegetables, if liked.

For red wine sauce, to serve with the sirloin, melt 2 tablespoons butter in a pan, add 6 finely chopped shallots, and cook until softened but not browned. Add 1¼ cups red wine and 1¼ cups beef or vegetable stock. Bring to a boil, reduce the heat, and simmer for 20–30 minutes, until reduced by half. Add 2 tablespoons chopped parsley and season with salt and black pepper. Remove from the heat and gradually whisk in 4 tablespoons butter. Add a little sugar if the sauce seems acidic.

moroccan stuffed lamb

Serves **8–10**
Preparation time
  15–20 minutes
Cooking time **50 minutes**

4½ lb **boned leg of lamb**
1 **onion**, cut in thick wedges
3 tablespoons **olive oil**
½ cup **lemon juice**
pepper

Moroccan stuffing
⅔ cup boiling **water**
¼ cup **couscous**
2 teaspoons **coriander seeds**
2 teaspoons **cumin seeds**
1 teaspoon **ground cinnamon**
3 tablespoons **olive oil**
⅓ cup **pine nuts**
½ cup **slivered almonds**
1 large **onion**, finely chopped
2 **garlic cloves**, crushed
1 teaspoon **dried mint**
¼ cup chopped **cilantro**
  leaves
⅓ cup **raisins**
salt and **black pepper**

Pour the boiling water over the couscous, stir, then let stand until absorbed. Heat the coriander and cumin seeds in a small pan until fragrant. Gzest to a powder, then mix with the cinnamon. Heat 1 tablespoon of the oil in a skillet, add the pine nuts and almonds, and fry until browned. Transfer to paper towels to drain. Add the remaining oil to the pan. When hot, add the onion and fry until soft. Stir in the garlic and spice mixture and fry for 2 minutes, then add the nuts, mint, cilantro, raisins, couscous, and salt and black pepper.

Open out the lamb, skin side down, on a work surface. Season inside with black pepper, then spread over the stuffing. If possible, tuck the flaps of the piece of lamb over the stuffing. Roll up the lamb into a neat sausage shape, then tie it securely with twine.

Put the onion wedges into a roasting pan in which the lamb will just fit. Place the lamb on top of the onion wedges and pour over the oil and lemon juice. Cook in a preheated oven at 475°F for 15 minutes, then reduce the temperature to 425°F, and cook for an additional 25 minutes, so that the lamb is pink in the center. Remove the lamb from the oven, cover, and let stand in a warm place for about 15 minutes before carving.

For lamb stuffed with figs & orange, omit the stuffing above and instead combine 1½ cups chopped dried figs, 2¾ cups fresh bread crumbs, 1 finely chopped onion, 2 teaspoons grated orange zest, scant ½ cup orange juice, ½ teaspoon ground cinnamon, and salt and black pepper. Stuff and cook the lamb as above. Serve garnished with sliced figs.

roasted goose with spiced apples

Serves **8**

Preparation time **35 minutes**

Cooking time **3¾ hours**

11–13 lb **oven-ready goose**,
  plus giblets

1 **onion**, halved

1 **carrot**

1 **celery rib**

5 cups **water**

4 tablespoons **butter**

1 large **onion**, chopped

1¾ cups chopped **dried figs**

3¾ cups **fresh bread crumbs**

2 tablespoons chopped
  parsley

2 tablespoons chopped
  thyme

1 **egg**

8 small **apples**, cored

16 whole **cloves**

2 tablespoons **packed light
  brown sugar**

½ teaspoon **ground allspice**

salt and **black pepper**

Put the giblets in a saucepan, discarding the liver. Add the halved onion, carrot, celery, and measured water. Bring to a boil, reduce the heat, and simmer gently for 1 hour. Strain the giblet stock and reserve.

Melt half the butter and fry the onion for 3 minutes. Remove from the heat and add 1¼ cups of the figs and the bread crumbs, parsley, thyme and egg. Season lightly and mix well. Pack half the stuffing into the neck end. Shape the remaining stuffing into 1 inch balls.

Tuck the skin flap under the bird and truss it, with the wings folded under the body and the legs tied together with twine. Place on a rack over a roasting pan. Roast the goose in a preheated oven at 350°F for 2¾ hours.

Cut a thin slice off the top of each apple and stud with 2 whole cloves. Combine the remaining figs, sugar, and allspice and pack into and on top of the apples. Melt the remaining butter and pour it over the apples.

Place the apples and stuffing in the oven 30 minutes before the end of the goose roasting time, basting the apples frequently with the butter. Test the goose to see if it is cooked (see page 14). Transfer to a warmed serving dish and add the spiced apples and stuffing balls. Keep warm.

Pour off all the fat from the roasting pan. Add 2½ cups reserved giblet stock, making up with water if necessary. Bring to a boil and season lightly with salt and black pepper. Strain and serve with the goose.

honey & citrus roast salmon

Serves **6**

Preparation time **10 minutes**,
  plus marinating

Cooking time **20 minutes**

2½ lb **side of salmon**
thinly pared zest and juice of
  1 orange
2 tablespoons **honey**
thinly pared zest of 1 **lemon**
2 tablespoons **butter**
salt and **black pepper**

To garnish
1 **lemon**, cut into wedges
a few **watercress sprigs**

Lay the salmon in a lightly greased baking sheet. Stir the orange juice into the honey and brush the mixture over the salmon. Cut the orange and lemon zest into thin strips and scatter them over the salmon. Let marinate in the refrigerator for 30 minutes.

Season the salmon with salt and black pepper, then bake in a preheated oven at 400°F for 20 minutes, until cooked through.

Transfer the salmon onto a serving platter and garnish with lemon wedges and watercress sprigs. Serve with new potatoes, if liked.

For salmon & cream cheese pâté, blend any leftover roast salmon with cream cheese in a food processor (or finely flake the salmon and stir in the cream cheese). You'll need 1 part cheese to 2 parts cooked salmon. Once well combined, stir in 2 tablespoons snipped chives, and season with salt and black pepper. Serve as a canapé on small triangles of toasted whole-wheat bread, if liked.

beef wellington

Serves **6**
Preparation time **30 minutes**
Cooking time about **1 hour**

3 lb **beef strip loin** (preferably cut from the middle of the short loin)
4 tablespoons **butter**
2 small **onions**, finely chopped
4¾ cups chopped **crenini mushrooms**
2 tablespoons **brandy**
1 lb **ready-to-use puff pastry**, defrosted if frozen
a little **flour**, for dusting
7 oz **smooth chicken pâté**
beaten **egg**, to glaze
salt and **black pepper**

Trim off the excess fat and season the beef. Melt the butter in a skillet and sear the beef on all sides. Transfer it to a roasting pan, reserving the fat in the skillet, and roast in a preheated oven at 400°F for 20 minutes. Leave to cool.

Fry the onions in the skillet for 5 minutes while the beef is cooking. Add the mushrooms and a little seasoning and fry until the moisture has evaporated. Add the brandy and fry for an additional 1 minute. Let cool.

Thinly roll out the pastry to a large rectangle on a lightly floured surface. Spread the top of the meat with the chicken pâté, then press a thick layer of the mushroom mixture over the top. Invert the beef on to the pastry and spread with the remaining mushrooms.

Brush the pastry with beaten egg and bring it up over the beef to enclose the meat completely, trimming off any bulky areas at the corners. Place, seam side down, on a lightly greased baking sheet and brush with more egg. Bake for 35 minutes, until deep golden. Let stand for 20 minutes before carving.

For individual beef Wellingtons, lightly sear four 5–6 oz strip loin steaks in a hot pan for 30 seconds on each side. Let cool. Divide 12 oz puff pastry into 4 and roll out each piece to a rectangle. Place a steak on each pastry rectangle. Season the steaks, then spread with 7 oz mushroom pâté. Enclose the meat in the pastry and continue as above, cooking for 25–30 minutes.

roasted duckling with clementines

Serves **4**

Preparation time
  20–25 minutes

Cooking time **2 hours**

5½ lb **oven-ready duckling**
½ teaspoon **ground allspice**
2 tablespoons **butter**
pared zest and juice of
  1 orange
2 **cinnamon sticks**, halved
4 **clementines**, peeled but left
  whole
1¾ cups fresh or frozen
  cranberries, defrosted if
  frozen
⅓ cup **packed light brown
  sugar**
2 teaspoons **white wine
  vinegar**
2 tablespoons **Cointreau**
salt and **black pepper**
bay leaves, to garnish
  (optional)

Pierce the duckling all over, except the breast area, to release the fat during cooking. Rub the skin with allspice and sprinkle with salt and black pepper. Place on a rack over a roasting pan and cook in a preheated oven at 425°F for 15 minutes. Reduce the temperature to 375°F and cook for an additional 1 hour.

Melt the butter in a small saucepan. Add the orange zest, cinnamon sticks, and whole clementines and cook for 1 minute. Place the clementines and orange zest around the duckling and pour over the remaining butter. Return to the oven for an additional 45 minutes.

Pour the orange juice and cranberries into the butter saucepan. Simmer gently for about 10 minutes, until the cranberries pop.

Put the duckling, cinnamon sticks, clementines, and orange zest in a serving dish. Garnish the dish with bay leaves (if liked) and keep warm. Drain the fat from the roasting pan, then add the cranberries and juice, sugar, vinegar, and Cointreau. Bring to a boil, stirring. Season to taste and serve with the duckling.

For roast duckling with kumquats, prepare the bird as above but rub with salt instead of allspice. Tuck 3 tarragon sprigs and 4 kumquats from a total weight of 8 oz inside the duckling and cook as above. A few minutes before it is cooked, halve the remaining kumquats and place in a pan with 1 tablespoon each orange juice and honey and 3 tablespoons sherry. Bring to a boil and cook gently for 2 minutes, stirring. Spoon on top of the duckling and serve.

feta & roast vegetable tart

Serves **6**
Preparation time **25 minutes**,
  plus chilling
Cooking time about **1 hour**

1 cup **self-rising flour**
½ cup **rolled oats**
6 tablespoons chilled **butter**,
  diced
about 2 tablespoons cold
  water
1 **eggplant**, sliced
1 **red bell pepper**, cored,
  seeded, and cut into thick
  strips
1 **onion**, cut into wedges
2 **zucchini**, cut into sticks
3 **tomatoes**, halved
2 **garlic cloves**, chopped
3 tablespoons **olive oil**
2 teaspoons chopped
  rosemary
4 oz **feta cheese**, crumbled
2 tablespoons freshly grated
  Parmesan cheese
salt and **black pepper**

Mix the flour and rolled oats in a bowl, then add the
butter and rub in until the mixture resembles fine bread
crumbs. Add the water and mix to a firm dough. Turn
out on to a lightly floured surface and knead briefly.

Roll out the pastry and line a 9 inch fluted tart pan,
pressing evenly into the sides. Prick the bottom with
a fork, chill for 15 minutes, then line with nonstick
parchment paper and pie weights or dried beans. Bake
in a preheated oven at 375°F for 10–15 minutes.
Remove the paper and macaroni or beans and return
to the oven for 5 minutes.

Mix the vegetables in a roasting pan. Add the garlic, oil
and rosemary, coating the vegetables evenly. Season
to taste. Roast at 400°F for 35 minutes or until the
vegetables are tender.

Fill the pastry shell with the cooked vegetables, scatter
the feta cheese over the top, and sprinkle with the
Parmesan. Return the tart to the oven for 10 minutes.

For roast pepper & haloumi tart, bake the pastry
shell as above, meanwhile roasting 2 large red,
2 large orange bell and 2 large yellow bell peppers,
all cut into thick strips, with the garlic, oil, rosemary,
and seasoning. Spread 6 tablespoons pesto over
the bottom of the pastry shell, then top with the bell
peppers. Sprinkle with 2 oz pitted black olives.
Omit the feta cheese and arrange 4 oz thinly sliced
haloumi cheese over the top. Bake for an additional
10 minutes as above.

pasta-packed baked red peppers

Serves **4**
Preparation time **20 minutes**
Cooking time **35–45 minutes**

4 **red bell peppers**, halved,
  cored, and seeded
1 cup cooked **mini macaroni**
2 **plum tomatoes**, chopped
1 cup grated **cheddar cheese**
2 **scallions**, sliced
2 tablespoons chopped
  parsley
3 tablespoons **olive oil**
salt and **black pepper**

Place the halved bell peppers in an ovenproof dish, hollows uppermost. Mix the macaroni, tomatoes, cheese, scallions, and parsley in a bowl. Spoon into the bell peppers, drizzle with the olive oil, and season to taste.

Bake in a preheated oven at 350°F for 35–45 minutes or until the macaroni filling is golden and bubbling.

For baked stuffed mushrooms, remove and finely chop the stalks from 4 large portobello mushrooms. Broil the mushrooms for 5 minutes, until just softened. Finely chop 1 small onion and mix with the chopped mushroom stalks, ½ cup cooked macaroni, ¼ cup chopped walnuts, 1 tablespoon chopped parsley, scant ¼ cup cubed cheddar cheese, and 1 tablespoon tomato paste. Season, then bind with a little beaten egg. Pile on top of the mushrooms, drizzle with a little olive oil, then cook under a preheated medium broiler for 15–20 minutes, until the top of the stuffing is crisp and has started to char at the edges.

melanzane parmigiana

Serves **6**

Preparation time **10 minutes**, plus draining

Cooking time **1 hour 25 minutes**

6 **aubergines**, cut lengthwise into thick slices

2 tablespoons **extra virgin olive oil**

2 cups grated **cheddar cheese**

½ cup freshly grated **Parmesan cheese**

salt

Tomato sauce

2 lb ripe **tomatoes**, roughly chopped

2 tablespoons **extra virgin olive oil**

2 **garlic cloves**, chopped

2 tablespoons chopped **basil**

1 teaspoon grated **lemon zest**

pinch of **sugar**

salt and **black pepper**

Sprinkle the eggplants with salt and let drain in a colander for 30 minutes. Wash well, drain, and pat dry on paper towels.

Bring all the ingredients for the tomato sauce to a boil. Cover and simmer for 30 minutes. Remove the lid and cook for an additional 20 minutes, until the sauce is thick. Adjust the seasoning.

Meanwhile brush the slices of eggplant with the oil and place on 2 large baking sheets. Roast at the top of a preheated oven at 400°F for 10 minutes on each side, until golden and tender.

Spoon a little tomato sauce into 6 lightly greased individual ovenproof dishes (or 1 lasagna dish) and top with a layer of eggplants and some cheddar. Continue the layers, finishing with the cheddar. Sprinkle the Parmesan over the top and bake at 400°F for 30 minutes, until bubbling and golden.

For eggplant layer pasta, slice, salt, rinse, and roast 3 sliced eggplants as above. Fry 1 chopped onion in 1 tablespoon olive oil for 5 minutes, then add 1½ tablespoons each chopped oregano and basil, 2½ cups sliced mushrooms and 3½ cups canned tomato sauce. Simmer for 10 minutes, then season. In an ovenproof dish, arrange 4–5 lasagna sheets, then add one-third of the tomato sauce, one-third of the eggplants, one-third of 18 oz sliced mozzarella and one-third of 1½ cups grated Gruyère. Repeat the layering twice. Cover with aluminium foil and bake at 375°F for 45 minutes. Remove the foil after 20 minutes to brown the top.

sesame roasted potatoes

Serves **4**
Preparation time **10 minutes**
Cooking time **1–1¼ hours**

4 **baking potatoes**,
  6–8 oz each, peeled and
  halved lengthwise
¼ cup **olive oil**
2 tablespoons **sesame seeds**
salt

Place the potatoes cut side down. Using a sharp knife, make cuts at ¼ inch intervals along the length of each potato almost through to the base, so that they just hold together.

Heat the oil in a roasting pan in a preheated oven at 400°F, until hot. Add the potatoes to the pan and spoon over the oil evenly. Sprinkle with a little salt, baste well, and roast the potatoes for 30 minutes.

Remove the potatoes from the oven, sprinkle with the sesame seeds, then return to the oven for an additional 30 minutes until golden brown and crisp.

For garlic & thyme roast potatoes, remove the potatoes from the oven after 30 minutes and, instead of sprinkling with sesame seeds, add 8 unpeeled garlic cloves and 10–12 thyme sprigs to the roasting pan. Cook for an additional 30 minutes, as above.

potatoes dauphinoise

Serves **4–6**

Preparation time **10 minutes**

Cooking time **1–1¼ hours**

1½–2 lb evenly shaped
  potatoes, peeled and thinly
  sliced
1 teaspoon grated **nutmeg**
1 **garlic clove**, crushed
1¼ cups **heavy cream**
⅔ cup grated **Gruyère** or
  cheddar cheese
salt and **black pepper**

Arrange the potatoes in layers in a well-greased ovenproof dish, sprinkling each layer with nutmeg, salt and black pepper.

Stir the crushed garlic clove into the cream and pour the cream over the potatoes. Sprinkle the cheese over the surface so that the potatoes are completely covered. Cover with aluminium foil and bake in a preheated oven at 350°F for 45 minutes.

Remove the foil and cook for an additional 15–30 minutes, or until the potatoes are cooked through and the cheese topping is crusty and golden brown.

For potato & leek bake, place 1 lb sliced leeks in the bottom of the dish before adding the layers of potatoes. Add the nutmeg, seasoning, cream, and garlic as above, then sprinkle ½ cup grated cheddar cheese mixed with ½ cup fresh breadcrumbs over the top.

roasted parsnips with thyme butter

Serves **4**
Preparation time **10 minutes**
Cooking time **40–45 minutes**

1¼ lb **baby parsnips**,
  scrubbed
1 tablespoon **extra virgin
  olive oil**
1 **garlic clove**, crushed
2 **thyme sprigs**, chopped
1 teaspoon grated **lemon zest**
pinch of **cayenne pepper**
pinch of **sea salt**

Toss the parsnips with the oil, garlic, thyme sprigs, lemon zest, cayenne pepper, and salt, and place in a roasting pan.

Bake in a preheated oven at 400°F for 40–45 minutes, stirring occasionally until golden and tender. Serve at once.

For roast butternut squash, cut a 2 lb squash in half lengthwise, remove the seeds and fibrous centers and cut into wedges. Toss with 2 tablespoons virgin olive oil, the leaves from 2 large thyme sprigs, and salt and black pepper, and place in a roasting pan. Bake at the top of a preheated oven at 425°F for 20–25 minutes, basting halfway through the cooking time, until the squash is soft and slightly browned. Serve drizzled with a little pumpkin seed oil.

brussels sprouts with chestnuts

Serves **10**
Preparation time **10 minutes**
Cooking time **6–10 minutes**

3 lb **Brussels sprouts**
4 tablespoons **butter**
4 cups halved cooked, peeled
  chestnuts
salt and **black pepper**

Remove the tough outer leaves and place the sprouts in a pan of boiling salted water. Cover and cook gently for 6–10 minutes, depending on their size, until just tender. (Be careful to avoid overcooking them, because overcooked sprouts have an unpleasant taste and smell.)

Meanwhile melt the butter in a saucepan and add the chestnuts. Heat gently until warmed through.

Drain the sprouts and stir into the warmed chestnuts. Season with a little salt and black pepper and serve.

For fried Brussels sprouts, halve 3 lb sprouts if large, cook in boiling water for 3 minutes, then drain. Melt 4 tablespoons butter or bacon fat in a skillet until sizzling, then add the sprouts and 2 crushed garlic cloves. Fry gently for 3 minutes. Season with grated nutmeg and salt and black pepper and sprinkle with a handful of lightly toasted slivered almonds before serving.

glazed baby carrots

Serves **6**
Preparation time **5 minutes**
Cooking time **15–20 minutes**

4 tablespoons **butter**
2 lb whole **baby carrots**, or
  young ones quartered
  lengthwise
generous pinch of **sugar**
juice of **1 orange**
salt and **black pepper**
parsley, roughly chopped,
  to garnish

Melt the butter in a saucepan, add the carrots and sugar, and season with salt and black pepper.

Pour in just enough water to cover the carrots and cook gently, uncovered, for 10–12 minutes or until the carrots are tender and the liquid has evaporated. As the water evaporates, add the orange juice. Serve garnished with the chopped parsley.

For carrots with ginger & orange butter, steam or boil 2 lb carrots for 10–12 minutes, until tender. Meanwhile, mix 4 tablespoons softened butter, 1 teaspoon grated fresh ginger, ½ teaspoon grated orange zest, ½ tablespoon orange juice, ½ teaspoon honey, 1 tablespoon chopped chervil, and salt and black pepper until smooth and evenly combined. Toss the cooked carrots in the spiced butter and serve at once.

roasted zucchini with shallots

Serves **4–6**
Preparation time **5 minutes**
Cooking time **40 minutes**

2 lb **zucchini**
6 **shallots**, quartered, with
   root left intact
¼ cup **olive oil**
1 tablespoon **pumpkin seed
   oil** (optional)
salt and **black pepper**

Cut the zucchini in half across the middle, then cut each piece in half again and then into quarters lengthwise to make batons.

Place the zucchini batons in a roasting pan and add the shallots. Mix the olive oil and the pumpkin seed oil, if using, and use to coat the zucchini batons and shallots. (If you don't want to use pumpkin seed oil, use 5 tablespoons olive oil in total instead.) Season with salt and black pepper and cook at the top of a preheated oven at 375°F for 40 minutes.

Baste the zucchini and shallots 2–3 times during cooking. Once cooked, the zucchini and shallots should be soft and speckled with brown.

For zucchini with orange, place 4½ medium (about 1½ lb) sliced zucchini and the grated zest and juice of 2 oranges in a saucepan. Cover tightly and simmer for about 4 minutes until the zucchini are tender. Add 2 tablespoons butter, season with black pepper, and toss until the zucchini are well coated.

braised red cabbage

Serves **8**
Preparation time **15 minutes**
Cooking time 2¼ **hours**

1 head **red cabbage**, about 4
tablespoons, finely shredded
50 g (2 oz) **fat salt pork**,
diced, or **butter**
2 **Bermuda onions**, thinly
sliced
¼ cup **packed brown sugar**
1¼ cups **tart apples**, peeled,
cored, and chopped
⅔ cup **chicken stock**
⅔ cup **red wine**
3 tablespoons **wine vinegar**
or **cider vinegar**
1 small **raw beet**, coarsely
grated
salt and **black pepper**

Put the cabbage in a large bowl. Cover with boiling water and set aside.

Using a large heavy pan, melt the butter. Add the onions and fry, stirring frequently, over moderate heat until soft and transparent. Stir in the sugar and continue to fry gently until the onions are caramelized and a rich golden color. Be careful to avoid letting the sugar burn.

Drain the cabbage thoroughly. Add it to the pan with the apples, stock, wine, and vinegar. Mix well. Season generously with salt and black pepper. Cover tightly and cook gently for 1½ hours, stirring occasionally.

Mix in the grated beet—this transforms the color—and continue to cook, covered, for 30 minutes longer, or until the cabbage is soft. Adjust the seasoning, if necessary, and serve very hot.

For crunchy red cabbage, proceed as above, adding 1 cup golden raisins at the same time as you add the apples. Just before serving, stir 1 cup blanched whole almonds into the red cabbage.

roasted sweet potatoes

Serves **6**
Preparation time **6 minutes**
Cooking time **50 minutes**

6 medium (about 2 lb) **sweet potatoes**, peeled and cut into even pieces
4 tablespoons **butter**
1 tablespoon **oil**
1 tablespoon **honey**
pinch of **ground ginger**
salt and **black pepper**

Drop the sweet potatoes into a saucepan of salted boiling water and simmer for 5 minutes, then drain.

Melt half the butter with the oil in a flameproof dish and stir in the honey and ginger. Add the sweet potatoes and toss in the honey mixture. Dot with the remaining butter, then season with salt and black pepper.

Cook in a preheated oven at 350°F for 40 minutes, or until the potatoes are tender. Brush with the glaze in the pan and turn occasionally during cooking.

For honey-roasted root vegetables, cut 5–6 medium carrots, 4 medium parsnips, and 3 medium turnips into ½ inch cubes. Heat 1 tablespoon oil in a skillet and quickly fry the vegetables until just colored. Transfer to a roasting pan, drizzle over 2 tablespoons honey, toss to coat evenly and roast in a preheated oven at 400°F for 1–1¼ hours, tossing frequently during cooking, until tender and well glazed.

onions stuffed with apple & stilton

Serves **4**
Preparation time **10 minutes**
Cooking time **50–55 minutes**

4 large **onions**, about 8 oz
   each
1 small **cooking apple**,
   peeled, cored, and chopped
1 cup **fresh bread crumbs**
½ cup finely crumbled **blue
   Stilton cheese**
½ bunch of **watercress**,
   trimmed and finely chopped
4 tablespoons **butter**
salt and **black pepper**

Cook the onions in boiling water for 15 minutes, until
they are just tender. Drain and let cool until they can
be handled.

Mix the apples with the bread crumbs and cheese, then
stir in the chopped watercress.

Remove the middle of each onion—this is easiest if
you gradually scoop out the layers of onion with a
teaspoon. Leave an unbroken shell about 2 layers
thick. Chop the scooped-out onion from 1 of the onions
(discarding the rest) and add to the cheese mixture. Mix
well and season to taste, then press the mixture into
the onion shells.

Stand the onions in an ovenproof dish and dot them
with the butter. Bake in a preheated oven at 350°Ffor
35–40 minutes, or until the stuffing is cooked through.

For roast onions in their skins, slice the stem ends
from 4 unpeeled onions, scrape the root ends, and
make a shallow cross in the core with a knife. Place
the onions in a greased roasting pan and cook in a
preheated oven at 400°F for about 1 hour, or until
tender but still firm when pierced with a skewer.
Remove from the oven, slip off the outer skins, and
place on a warmed serving dish. Season with salt
and black pepper. Squeeze slightly to open the
centers and push a pat of butter into each onion.
Garnish with watercress or parsley sprigs.

camembert leeks

Serves **4**
Preparation time **15 minutes**
Cooking time **18–20 minutes**

1½ lb **baby leeks**
1½ tablespoons **butter**
½ tablespoon finely chopped
  onion
2 tablespoons **all-purpose**
  flour
⅔ cup **milk**
2 oz **Camembert cheese**,
  zest removed, chopped
salt and **black pepper**
chopped **parsley**, to garnish

Cook the leeks in boiling salted water for 8 minutes, or until tender. Drain and place in a shallow heatproof dish. Keep warm.

Melt the butter in a pan, add the onion, and fry until soft. Stir in the flour and cook for 1 minute. Gradually blend in the milk. Heat, stirring, until the sauce thickens.

Add the Camembert and heat gently, stirring, until it has melted. Season to taste, then pour the sauce over the leeks. Garnish with parsley and serve immediately.

For cauliflower with Stilton, cook the florets of 1 head cauliflower in boiling salted water for about 10 minutes or until tender. Drain and transfer to a warmed ovenproof serving dish. Make the cheese sauce as above, omitting the onion and replacing the Camembert with ¾ cup crumbled blue Stilton. Pour the sauce over the cauliflower and top with 2 tablespoons whole-wheat bread crumbs. Cook under a preheated medium broiler until golden brown.

cold baked ham

Serves **10–12**
Preparation time **5 minutes**,
   plus soaking
Cooking time **2 hours**
   25 minutes–3 hours

5½–8½ lb **ham joint**, either on
   the bone or boned and rolled
2 **bay leaves**
½ cup **raw brown sugar**
3 tablespoons **ginger
   marmalade**
⅔ cup **ginger ale**

Place the ham in a large saucepan of cold water and let soak for 2–12 hours, depending on the amount of salt in the cure (soak overnight if in doubt).

Drain the ham, then weigh it and calculate the cooking time based on 25 minutes per 1 lb, plus 20 minutes. For a joint over 6½ lb, allow 20 minutes per 1 lb, plus 20 minutes. Return it to the pan and cover with fresh cold water. Add the bay leaves and 2 tablespoons of the sugar and bring to a boil. Cover, reduce the heat, and simmer for half the calculated cooking time.

Remove the ham from the water and strip off the skin. Stand the joint on a large sheet of aluminium foil in a roasting pan and score the fat diagonally in a trellis pattern. Mix the marmalade and remaining sugar and spread over the fat. Pour the ginger ale around the joint and enclose in the foil, sealing the edges firmly.

Bake in a preheated oven at 375°F for the remaining cooking time. During cooking, baste the ham with the ginger ale, then rewrap in the foil. About 20 minutes before the end of the cooking time, fold back the foil, baste again, and return to the oven. Remove and let cool overnight.

For cranberry baked ham, use 3 tablespoons ready-to-use cranberry and orange sauce instead of the marmalade. Omit the ginger ale and pour ⅔ cup dry hard cider around the joint.

festive game pie

Serves **8**

Preparation time **45 minutes**, plus cooling

Cooking time **1½ hours**

14½ oz **sausage-meat**

2 **onions**, finely chopped

2 teaspoons chopped **thyme**

6 tablespoons **butter**

13 oz lean **turkey**, diced

4 **pigeon breasts**, sliced

1 lb **pheasant**, diced

2 **celery ribs**, thinly sliced

3 **garlic cloves**, crushed

3 tablespoons **all-purpose flour**

3¾ cups **game** or **chicken stock**

2 cups halved cooked, peeled **chestnuts**

milk, to glaze

salt and **black pepper**

Flaky pastry

3 cups **all-purpose flour**

8 tablespoons (1 stick) **butter**, diced

½ cup diced **lard**

2 teaspoons iced **water**

pinch of **salt**

Place the flour and salt in a bowl, add the fats, and rub in with the fingertips until the mixture resembles coarse bread crumbs. Use a round-bladed knife to stir in the measured water until the mixture starts to bind. Bring to a dough, adding a little more water if it feels dry. Lightly knead on a floured surface until smooth. Wrap and chill until required.

Combine the sausage-meat with 1 chopped onion and a little thyme and shape into 18 small balls. Melt 2 tablespoons of the butter in a skillet, fry the meatballs until golden, then drain. Season all the other meats and fry, in batches, until golden, adding more butter if needed. Drain.

Melt the rest of the butter in the skillet and fry the remaining onion and the celery and garlic. Blend in the flour, add the stock, and bring to a boil. Cook for 4–5 minutes.

Mix all the meats and chestnuts in a 2-quart pie dish and pour over enough of the liquid to come to within ¾ inch of the rim. Let cool.

Roll out the pastry on a lightly floured surface until 2 inches larger than the pie pan. Cut a 1 inch strip from around the edges and place it on the dampened rim of the pan. Brush with milk, cover with the pastry lid, fluting the edges with the back of a knife, and score a cross in the center. Use the pastry trimmings to make leaves for the top, then brush with more milk. Bake in a preheated oven at 375°F for 1 hour, until deep golden, covering with foil if the pastry begins to get too brown.

chicken liver pâté

Serves **4–6**
Preparation time **20 minutes**,
  plus cooling and chilling
Cooking time **10 minutes**

1⅔ cups **unsalted butter**
2 **garlic cloves**, crushed
1 lb **chicken livers**, cores
  removed, roughly chopped
⅓–½ cup **brandy**, according to
  taste
salt and **black pepper**

Melt 4 tablespoons of the butter in a large skillet over moderate heat until foaming. Reduce the heat, add the garlic and stir for 2–3 minutes, until it is softened but not colored.

Add the chicken livers, increase the heat to moderate and toss vigorously for 5–8 minutes, until the livers are browned on the outside, but still remain pink-tinged in the center.

Pour in the brandy and stir well. Let the mixture bubble for 1–2 minutes, then transfer to a food processor or blender. Cut all but 4 tablespoons of the remaining butter into pieces and add to the machine. Work the mixture to a smooth puree and season to taste.

Turn the mixture into individual custard cups or a large serving bowl and smooth the surface. Melt the remaining butter in a clean pan, then pour over the surface of the pâté. Let stand until cold, then cover and chill overnight in the refrigerator. Serve the pâté chilled, accompanied by triangles of hot whole-wheat toast, if liked.

For Stilton & walnut pâté, melt 2 tablespoons butter in a pan, add 3½ tablespoons flour, and cook for 1 minute. Gradually add 1 cup milk, mixing well, then bring to a boil, stirring constantly, and cook until smooth and thickened. Remove from the heat, add 1 cup crumbled blue Stilton, and stir until melted. Add ⅓ cup chopped walnuts and 2 teaspoons each chopped parsley and brandy, and season. Serve chilled, garnished with some walnut pieces and small parsley sprigs.

winter salad

Serves **8**

Preparation time **20 minutes**

2 **green apples**, cored and sliced

2 **red apples**, cored and sliced

2 **Bosc pears**, peeled, cored, and sliced

2 tablespoons **lemon juice**

1 stalk **celery**, sliced

⅓–½ cup **shelled walnuts**

4 **scallions**, finely sliced

1 bunch **watercress**

⅓ cup **French dressing**

Place the apples, pears, and lemon juice in a large bowl. Stir lightly but thoroughly to mix, then pour off the excess lemon juice.

Add the celery, walnuts, scallions, and watercress.

Pour the French dressing over the salad. Toss lightly but thoroughly, then turn into a salad bowl, cover, and chill in the refrigerator until required.

For spinach & Roquefort salad, place 12 oz trimmed baby spinach leaves and ⅔ cup roughly chopped walnuts in a salad bowl. To make the dressing, use a fork to mash 2 oz Roquefort cheese with ⅔ cup crème fraîche (or ⅓ cup reduced-fat sour cream mixed with ⅓ cup whipping cream) and a little milk until smooth. Add the mashed mixture to the salad bowl, toss the ingredients thoroughly, and serve at once.

roasted vegetable & bread salad

Serves **4**

Preparation time **25 minutes**, plus cooling

Cooking time **50 minutes**

1 large **eggplant**, cubed

4 **zucchini**, cubed

2 **red bell peppers**, cored, seeded, and sliced

4 **garlic cloves**

about ¼ cup **extra virgin olive oil**

4 firm ripe **tomatoes**, diced

6 slices day-old **bread**, diced

2 tablespoons boiling **water**

handful of small **basil leaves**

salt and **black pepper**

Dressing

½ cup **extra virgin olive oil**

2 tablespoons **red wine vinegar**

pinch of **sugar**

Toss the eggplant, zucchini, bell peppers, and garlic with the olive oil and place in a large roasting pan. Bake in a preheated oven at 425°F for 50 minutes. Remove the pan from the oven and stir in the tomatoes, adding a little extra oil if necessary.

Whisk together the oil, vinegar, sugar, and a little seasoning. Stir 3 tablespoons of the dressing into the vegetables and let cool.

Place the bread in a bowl. Add the measured boiling water to the remaining dressing and stir into the bread, then let soak for 10 minutes.

Add the bread to the vegetables with the basil and season to taste before serving.

For pancetta & cannellini bean salad, lightly fry 4 oz pancetta cubes in a nonstick skillet for 2–3 minutes, turning occasionally. When cooked, turn the pancetta and cooking juices into a bowl containing 3 cups canned cannellini beans, drained, and 4 chopped scallions. Toss well, season to taste, and serve warm or cold.

traditional christmas pudding

Serves **12**
Preparation time **30 minutes**
Cooking time **9–12 hours**

1 cup **self-raising flour**
3¾ cups **fresh white bread crumbs**
1 cup **currants**
1 cup **sultanas**
¾ cup chopped **pitted dates**
1¾ cups **seedless raisins**
¾ cup **lard**
¼ cup **chopped peel**
⅓ cup chopped **blanched almonds**
1 small **apple**, peeled, cored, and grated
grated zest and juice of
1 small **orange**
½ teaspoon **ground allspice**
¼ teaspoon grated **nutmeg**
½ teaspoon **salt**
3 **eggs**
¼ cup **brown ale** or **hard cider**
1¼ cups **packed dark brown sugar**
3–4 tablespoons **brandy**, to serve

Place all the pudding ingredients in a large bowl and stir well to mix.

Grease liberally a 1¼ quart heatproof bowl and a ½ quart heatproof bowl. Spoon the mixture into each bowl until just over three-quarters full, then cover with circles of greased wax paper, then with aluminium foil. Fold a pleat in the center and tie twine securely around the rim.

Place in the top of a steamer or double boiler, or put in a large pan and pour in boiling water to come halfway up the sides. Boil for 6–8 hours, depending on size, adding extra boiling water as necessary. Remove the bowls from the pans and let stand overnight to cool.

Remove the coverings and recover with fresh greased wax paper and foil. Store in a cool, dry, dark place for up to 6 months.

Reboil the puddings for 3–4 hours, depending on size, then turn out onto a warm dish. Warm the brandy, pour over the pudding, and set alight. Serve with crème anglaise (see below) or brandy butter, rum butter, or brandy cream (see page 84).

For crème anglaise, to serve 6, heat 1¼ cups milk with 1¼ cups light cream in a heavy pan and bring slowly to a boil. Whisk 6 egg yolks and 2 tablespoons superfine sugar in a bowl until thick and pale, then add 2 teaspoons vanilla extract. Pour the milk and cream mixture over the yolk and sugar mixture, whisking well. Cook over moderate heat for 5–10 minutes, stirring constantly, until the sauce thickly coats the back of the spoon. Serve warm.

last-minute christmas pudding

Serves **8**

Preparation time
  30 minutes, plus standing

Cooking time **6–7 hours**

½ cup **packed dark sugar**

4½ cups **fresh white bread crumbs**

½ cup **lard**

pinch of **salt**

1 teaspoon **ground allspice**

1¼ cups **golden raisins**

1¼ cups **seedless raisins**

¾ cup **currants**

¼ cup chopped **candied peel**

3 tablespoons finely chopped **blanched almonds**

1 large **cooking apple**, peeled, cored, and finely chopped

finely grated zest and juice of ½ **lemon**

1 **egg**, beaten

⅔ cup **Guinness** or **milk stout**

about ⅓ cup **milk**

confectioners' sugar, for dusting

2 tablespoons **brandy**, to serve

Put the dry ingredients, dried fruit, candied peel, and almonds into a large bowl and stir well to mix. Add the apple with the lemon zest and juice, egg, and Guinness or milk stout and stir well. Add enough milk to make a soft dropping consistency.

Turn into a greased 1¼ quart heatproof bowl. Cover the top of the pudding with a circle of greased wax paper, then with aluminium foil. Fold a pleat in the center and tie twine around the rim. Let stand overnight.

Place the bowl in the top of a steamer or double boiler, or in a large pan of gently bubbling water, and steam for 4–5 hours, adding extra boiling water as necessary.

Remove the bowl carefully from the pan and let cool completely. Discard the foil and wax paper. Replace with fresh wax paper and foil if you intend to store the pudding, but it doesn't need to mature and can be made just before Christmas.

Steam again for 2 hours before serving. Dust with confectioners' sugar and decorate with a holly leaf, if liked. Warm the brandy, pour over the pudding, and set alight. Serve with crème anglaise (see page 80) or brandy butter, rum butter, or brandy cream (see page 84).

For individual Christmas puddings, make the pudding mixture as described above and use to fill 8 individual ⅔ cup heatproof bowls. Cover as above, then steam for just 2 hours. Steam again for about 1 hour before serving.

brandy butter

Serves **6**
Preparation time
10–15 minutes

¾ cup (1½ sticks) **unsalted butter**, softened
1⅛ cups **confectioners' sugar**, sifted
thinly grated zest of ½ **orange**, plus a few thinly pared strips to garnish
2 tablespoons **brandy**

Put the butter in a bowl and, using an electric mixer, beat until light and fluffy. Gradually beat in the confectioners' sugar, then beat in the orange zest and the brandy.

Turn the brandy butter into a serving bowl and chill in the refrigerator until quite firm. Serve garnished with thinly pared strips of orange zest.

For rum butter, beat the butter as above, using 8 tablespoons (1 stick) unsalted softened butter, ¼ cup packed brown sugar and 2 tablespoons light rum.

For brandy cream, whip 1¼ cups whipping cream with 1 tablespoon confectioners' sugar, using an electric mixer, until soft peaks form. Add 2 tablespoons brandy (or Cointreau, if preferred) and stir to combine.

bombe noël

Serves **6–8**

Preparation time **20 minutes**, plus soaking and freezing

Cooking time **10 minutes**

½ cup chopped **candied cherries**, plus extra whole ones to decorate (optional)

½ cup chopped **dried cranberries**

½ cup chopped **candied pineapple**

½ cup drained and chopped **preserved ginger**

⅓ cup **seedless raisins**

¼ cup **brandy**

3 **egg yolks**

⅓ cup **superfine sugar**

1¼ cups **light cream**

⅔ cup **heavy cream**

⅓ cup chopped toasted **almonds**, plus extra whole ones to decorate (optional)

candied ginger, chopped, to decorate (optional)

Place the cherries, cranberries, pineapple, preserved ginger, and raisins in a bowl. Pour the brandy over and let soak for 1 hour.

Beat the yolks and sugar until thoroughly combined. Bring the light cream just to a boil, remove from the heat, and stir gradually into the yolk mix. Transfer to a heatproof bowl over a pan of simmering water and cook gently, stirring constantly, until the custard is thick enough to coat the back of a spoon. Strain into a bowl and let cool, stirring occasionally.

Whip the heavy cream until it stands in soft peaks, then fold in the cold custard. Freeze in a rigid container, covered, for 2–3 hours, until half-frozen. Stir in the fruit, brandy and chopped almonds. Place in a 1 quart foil heatproof bowl and level the surface.

Cover the bowl with aluminium foil, then wrap in a plastic bag. Seal and freeze for up to 3 months. To defrost and serve, unwrap the bowl and invert onto a serving plate. Rub with a cloth wrung out in very hot water until the bombe drops out. Place in the refrigerator for 30 minutes. Decorate with some whole candied cherries and toasted almonds and a few pieces of chopped candied ginger, if liked.

For Christmas pudding ice cream, replace the candied cherries, cranberries, candied pineapple, ginger, and raisins with 2¼ cups dried mixed luxury fruit. Add 1 teaspoon each ground allspice and ground cinnamon to the frozen cream and custard mixture with the brandy-soaked fruit and the almonds. Omit the candied cherry, toasted almond, and ginger decoration.

ricotta & candied fruit slice

Serves **8**
Preparation time **20 minutes**
Cooking time **25 minutes**

12 oz **ready-to-use puff pastry**, defrosted if frozen
a little **flour**, for dusting
confectioners' sugar, for dusting

Filling
8 oz **firm ricotta cheese**
⅓ cup finely chopped **mixed candied fruit**
2 oz finely chopped **dark chocolate**
grated zest of 1 **lemon**
beaten **egg**, to glaze
¼ cup **slivered almonds**

Roll out the pastry on a lightly floured surface until it is ½ inch thick and an 8 x 12 inch rectangle. Place the rectangle on a baking sheet lined with parchment paper.

Make the filling. Beat the ricotta until it is smooth and then stir in the candied fruit, chocolate, and lemon zest. Spread the mixture down the center of the pastry, leaving a 2 inch border down each side.

Score the pastry lightly along each side of the filling and fold over the pastry sides to cover the edges of the filling. Brush the pastry with beaten egg and sprinkle over the slivered almonds, pressing them down lightly.

Bake in a preheated oven at 400°F for 25 minutes, until risen and golden, then remove from the oven and let cool.

Dust the tart generously with confectioners' sugar before serving cut in slices.

For ricotta & date slice, omit the candied fruit and lemon zest and stir 1 cup chopped, pitted dates and the grated zest of 1 orange into the cheese, together with the chocolate. Continue as above.

clementine & mincemeat tart

Serves **6**

Preparation time **20 minutes**, plus chilling

Cooking time **33–40 minutes**

⅔ cup **all-purpose flour**

⅔ cup **whole-wheat flour**

6 tablespoons chilled **butter**, diced

½ cup **ground almonds**

2 tablespoons **superfine sugar**

grated zest of 1 **orange**

1 **egg**, beaten

1¼ cups **luxury mincemeat**

3 **clementines**, segmented

milk, to glaze

confectioners' sugar, for dusting

Put both the flours in a bowl, add the butter, and rub in with the fingertips until the mixture resembles fine bread crumbs. Stir in the almonds, sugar, and orange zest, then add the egg and mix to a firm dough.

Knead the dough briefly on a lightly floured surface, then roll out and use to line a 9 inch loose-bottom fluted tart pan. Prick the bottom with a fork, chill for 15 minutes, then line with nonstick parchment paper and add pie weights or dried beans. Bake in a preheated oven at 375°F for 10–15 minutes. Remove the paper and weights or beans and return to the oven for an additional 5 minutes.

Mix the mincemeat and clementine segments, then fill the pastry shell. Gather up the pastry trimmings, reroll, and cut into differently sized stars. Place on the topping, brush with milk and dust with confectioners' sugar.

Bake at the above temperature for 18–20 minutes until the fruit is caramelized and the stars look baked. Dust with confectioners' sugar and serve warm or cold.

For cranberry & mincemeat latticed tart, bake the pastry shell as above. Fill with the mincemeat mixed with 1¾ cups fresh or frozen cranberries instead of the clementines. Reroll the pastry trimmings thinly and cut into ½ in wide strips. Dampen the edges of the pastry shell and, twisting it slightly, lay a pastry strip across one side of the tart, pressing the edges to seal. Lay a second twisted strip of pastry at right angles to the first. Continue attaching twisted pastry strips alternately at right angles. Trim off excess pastry and cook as above.

frosted grapes

Serves **6–8**

Preparation time **20 minutes**, plus setting

½ bunch of **green seedless grapes**

½ bunch of **red seedless grapes**

a few **cape gooseberries** (optional), with some leaves left intact

1 cup **confectioners' sugar**

4–5 teaspoons **orange** or **lime juice**

¼ cup **superfine sugar**

Wash the grapes and the cape gooseberries (if using), then pat dry with paper towels. Snip the grapes into tiny bunches of 2–3 grapes.

Sift the confectioners' sugar into a bowl, then gradually mix in the fruit juice to make a smooth, thick frosting.

Dip the grapes a bunch at a time into the frosting, then dip in the cape gooseberries. Arrange the grapes and cape gooseberries on a wire rack set over a baking sheet. Let stand in a cool place for 1 hour or until hardened.

Sprinkle the grapes and cape gooseberries with superfine sugar before serving.

For candied fruits, use a selection of fruit with edible skins, for example small bunches of grapes or red currants, or strawberries, plums, and pears. Brush lightly with beaten egg white and place in a colander set over a large bowl. Sprinkle the fruit generously with granulated sugar and let stand until the sugar has hardened.

winter dried fruit salad

Serves **6**

Preparation time **5 minutes**, plus soaking

Cooking time **10–15 minutes**

1 cup **dried apricots**
½ cup **dried prunes**
⅔ cup **dried figs**
¾ cup **dried apples**
2½ cups **apple juice**
2 tablespoons **Calvados** or **brandy**
3 tablespoons roughly chopped **walnuts**

Place the dried fruits in a bowl with the apple juice and let soak overnight.

Transfer the fruits and juice to a saucepan and simmer for 10–15 minutes.

Turn into a glass bowl and pour over the Calvados or brandy. Sprinkle with the walnuts. Serve warm or cold with crème fraîche or cream.

For fruit & nut crumble, soak and simmer the dried fruits as above, then turn into an ovenproof dish. Omit the Calvados or brandy and walnuts and make a crumble topping instead. Rub 6 tablespoons unsalted butter into 1⅓ cups whole-wheat flour until the mixture resembles bread crumbs. Stir in ¼ cup packed dark brown sugar and ⅓ cup chopped hazelnuts. Sprinkle over the fruit mixture and bake in a preheated oven at 400°F for 25–30 minutes.

poached pears in cassis

Serves **6**
Preparation time **10 minutes**
Cooking time **50 minutes**

1¼ cups **red wine**
⅔ cup **cassis**
2 **cinnamon sticks**
2 strips **lemon zest**
2 strips **orange zest**
1¼ cups **water**
6 firm, ripe **pears**, peeled
⅔ cup **Greek yogurt**
2 tablespoons **Greek honey**
1 teaspoon **ground cinnamon**

Place the wine, cassis, cinnamon sticks, citrus peel, and measured water in a saucepan and bring to a boil. Add the pears, cover the pan, and simmer gently for about 40 minutes, until the pears are cooked through but not mushy.

Remove the pears with a slotted spoon and place in a serving dish. Bring the poaching liquid to a rolling boil and simmer until it is reduced by half and is thick and syrupy. Pour over the pears and let cool.

Combine the yogurt, honey, and cinnamon and set aside to let the flavors develop. Serve the pears at room temperature with a spoonful of the cinnamon cream for each serving.

For poached figs, replace the pears with 12 large, firm, ripe figs. Cook the figs in the syrup as above for 10 minutes, until they are dark red and softened (don't overcook or the figs will fall apart). Remove the figs from the syrup and continue as above. This recipe serves 4.

ginger & hazelnut ice cream

Serves **4**

Preparation time **5 minutes**, plus freezing

1¼ cups **heavy cream**

2 tablespoons **milk**

¼ cup **confectioners' sugar**, sifted

2 tablespoons drained and finely chopped **preserved ginger**

4 teaspoons **ginger syrup**

2–4 tablespoons finely chopped **hazelnuts**, plus extra to decorate

Whip the cream and milk lightly, then fold in the confectioners' sugar. Pour into a shallow freezer container, cover, and freeze for about 45 minutes, until the ice cream has frozen around the sides of the container.

Turn into a chilled bowl and whisk until smooth. Stir in the ginger, syrup, and hazelnuts.

Return the ice cream to the container, cover and freeze until firm. Transfer to the refrigerator about 20 minutes before serving, to soften.

Scoop into dishes and sprinkle with a few extra chopped hazelnuts to serve.

For maple & pecan ice cream, omit the preserved ginger, ginger syrup, and hazelnuts, and stir in ⅔ cup finely chopped pecans and 4 teaspoons pure maple syrup instead. Continue as above.

champagne strawberry cup

Serves **6**
Preparation time **5 minutes**

¾ cup **strawberry liqueur**
  (such as fraises des bois),
  chilled
1 bottle non-vintage **dry
  Champagne** or **dry
  sparkling white wine**,
  chilled
¾ cup sliced **strawberries**

Pour the liqueur into a large pitcher. Gradually add the Champagne or sparkling wine, stirring very gently so as to avoid losing the bubbles.

Divide the strawberry slices among individual Champagne flutes and fill up with the strawberry-flavored Champagne. Serve at once.

For kir royale, pour chilled dry Champagne or sparkling white wine into Champagne flutes. Slowly add 2 tablespoons crème de cassis to each glass so that it gently mingles with the Champagne to give a pale pink glass of fizz.

For classic Champagne cocktail, place a sugar cube in each Champagne flute. Saturate it with Angostura bitters, then add 2 tablespoons brandy to each glass. Fill with chilled Champagne.

glühwein

Serves **6**
Preparation time **5 minutes**
Cooking time **10–12 minutes**

2 **lemons**, sliced
1 **orange**, sliced
1 bottle **red wine**
⅔ cup **sugar**
8 whole **cloves**
2 **cinnamon sticks**
1¼ cups **brandy**

Place the slices of 1 lemon in a saucepan with the sliced orange, red wine, sugar, cloves, and cinnamon sticks. Simmer gently for 10 minutes, then reduce the heat and add the brandy.

Serve the glühwein in small cups or heatproof glasses with the remaining slices of lemon.

For party glögg, to serve 15–20, place the zest of 1 orange, 20 lightly crushed cardamom pods, 20 whole cloves, and 2 cinnamon sticks in a piece of muslin, tie securely, and add to a saucepan with 1 bottle red wine, 1 bottle port or Madeira, 1¼ cups blanched almonds, and 1¾ cups raisins. Heat at just below boiling point for 25 minutes, stirring occasionally. Place 8–12 oz sugar cubes on a wire rack over the pan. Warm 1¼ cups brandy and pour evenly over the sugar cubes. Set the cubes alight—they will melt through the wire rack into the wine. Stir the glögg and remove the spice bag. Serve hot, with a few raisins and almonds in each cup.

centerpiece cakes

rich christmas cake

Serves **16**

Preparation time **45 minutes**, plus cooling

Cooking time **3–3½ hours**

1 cup **self-rising flour**

1⅔ cups **all-purpose flour**

¼ teaspoon **salt**

1 teaspoon **ground allspice**

½ teaspoon **ground cinnamon**

½ teaspoon **ground nutmeg**

1 cup (2 sticks) **butter**

1¼ cups **packed dark brown** or **raw brown sugar**

2 teaspoons **molasses**

5 **eggs**

¼ cup **medium-dry sherry** or strained cold **tea**

1½ cups teaspoons **vanilla extract**

1¾ cups **currants**

1¾ cups **golden raisins**

1¾ cups roughly chopped **prunes** or **dates**

1¾ cups **seedless raisins**

½ cup **chopped candied peel**

½ cup **ground almonds**

⅓ cup halved **candied cherries**

finely grated zest of 1 **lemon**

3–4 tablespoons **brandy**

Grease and line a 9 inch round or 8 inch square cake pan, using a double thickness of greased wax paper. Line the outside with several thicknesses of brown craft paper, standing at least 2 inches above the top of the pan.

Sift the flours into a bowl with the salt, allspice, cinnamon, and nutmeg. In another large bowl, cream the butter with the sugar until light. Beat in the molasses.

Lightly beat together the eggs, sherry or tea, and vanilla extract. Gradually beat half the egg mixture into the creamed mixture. Fold in one-third of the mixed flours. Conpanue to add the egg and flour mixtures alternately. Mix in all the remaining ingredients except the brandy. Turn into the prepared pan and smooth the top.

Bake in a preheated oven at 275°F for about 3–3½ hours until a skewer inserted into the center of the cake comes out clean. Cover the cake with a double layer of wax paper if it starts to brown too much during cooking.

Let the cake cool in the pan before turning out on to a wire rack to cool completely. Prick all over with a fine skewer and spoon brandy over the cake. Store the cake in an airtight container and leave to mature for about 1 month before using.

For iced rich Christmas cake, brush the cake all over with smooth apricot jam, then cover with 2¼ lb marzipan (use half this quantity if you want to cover only the top of the cake). Ice the whole cake with 2–3 coats of thin royal icing (see page 10).

santa's bag

Serves **10**

Preparation time **25 minutes**

7 x 4 inch **store-bought rich fruit cake**

2 tablespoons **smooth apricot jam**

1½ lb **red ready-to-use fondant**

selection of **wrapped chocolates** and **chocolate coins**

3 oz **white ready-to-use fondant**

confectioners' sugar, for dusting

Put the cake on a serving plate or cake board and spread the sides with the apricot jam, reserving a little.

Knead the red fondant until softened, then roll out thinly on a surface lightly dusted with confectioners' sugar. Cut out 2 rectangles, 7½ x 6½ inches, and press them on to the long sides of the cake. Reroll the trimmings and cut out two 5½ inch squares. Press them on to the short ends of the cake.

Smooth the fondant over the cake and press the fondant seams together. Don't worry if the fondant sags down the sides—this will make the bag look more interesting. Smooth the top edge of the fondant to give a wavy effect, then fill the top of the bag with sweets and coins. Roll out the white fondant and stamp out tiny stars or holly leaves. Stick them onto the sides of the bag with a little jam.

For Madeira cake Santa's bag, use two 9 oz store-bought Madeira cake bars instead of the fruit cake. Sandwich the long edges together with jam or Vanilla Butter cream (see page 120), then decorate as above.

christmas wreath cake

Serves **16**
Preparation time **1 hour**

9 inch **Rich Christmas Cake**
(see page 106)
4 tablespoons **smooth
apricot jam**
2 lb **white marzipan**
2 lb **white ready-to-use
fondant**
red, **dark green**, **citrus green**,
and **light green food
colorings**
3 oz **dark chocolate**, broken
into pieces
confectioners' sugar, for
dusting

Brush the cake with 3 tablespoons apricot jam. Set aside 6 oz marzipan and use the rest to cover the cake, smoothing it over the top and down the sides. Trim to fit. Place the cake on a cake board.

Knead the fondant lightly and roll out on a work surface dusted with confectioners' sugar until large enough to cover the cake. Dampen the marzipan, then lift the fondant carefully over the cake, supporpang it with a rolling pin. Smooth over the top, then down the sides. Trim off the excess icing. Color icing trimmings with red food coloring to make holly berries. Let dry on parchment paper.

Wrap a rolling pin with nonstick parchment paper. Melt the chocolate in a heatproof bowl over a pan of gently simmering water. Drizzle the melted chocolate quickly back and forth across the rolling pin. Let set.

Divide the reserved marzipan into 3, color each third a different shade of green, and place in plastic bags to prevent them from drying out. Lightly knead two green shades together to give a marbled effect. Roll out thinly on a surface lightly dusted with confectioners' sugar and cut out ivy leaves. Mark with veins and twist slightly.

Roll out the remaining colored marzipan and cut out light green and dark green holly leaves. Mark with veins and shape. Let all the marzipan shapes to dry overnight on parchment paper.

Use a dampened paintbrush to moisten the fondant so you can attach the leaves and berries in a wreath shape. Peel the chocolate off the paper, break into "twigs" and place on the wreath.

epiphany ring

Serves **12**

Preparation time **15–20 minutes,** plus rising

Cooking time **20–25 minutes**

4 cups **white bread flour**

1 teaspoon **salt**

grated zest of 1 **orange**

grated zest of 1 **lemon**

⅔ cup **superfine sugar**

1½ teaspoons **active dry yeast**

76 tablespoons **butter,** melted

2 **eggs,** beaten, plus extra **yolk** to glaze

¾ cup **water**

½ cup **whole candied peel**

⅔ cup **candied cherries**

1 cup **slivered, blanched almonds**

1 tablespoon cold **water**

1 cup **confectioners' sugar**

4–5 teaspoons **lemon juice**

Put the flour in a large bowl, then stir in the salt, zests, sugar, and yeast. Add the butter and beaten eggs, then gradually mix in enough warm water to make a soft dough. Knead well until the dough is smooth and elastic. Put back into the bowl and cover with greased plastic wrap. Let stand in a warm place to rise for 1¼ hours or until doubled in size.

Turn out onto a lightly floured surface and knead well. Roughly chop the candied peel, cherries, and almonds. Reserve one-third of the mixture, then gradually knead the remainder into the dough.

Shape into a thick rope 20 inches long and push the ends together to make a ring. Place on a greased baking sheet. Stand a greased bowl in the center of the ring to keep the hole and cover loosely with greased plastic wrap. Let stand to rise for 30 minutes or until half as big again.

Remove the bowl, brush with yolk mixed with the water, and bake in a preheated oven at 400°F for 20–25 minutes, until the bread is golden brown and sounds hollow when tapped. Cover with aluminium foil if overbrowning. Transfer to a wire rack to cool.

Sift the confectioners' sugar into a bowl, then gradually mix in the lemon juice to make a smooth, pouring icing. Drizzle over the bread in random lines. Sprinkle with the reserved fruit and nuts, then let stand to set.

For epiphany ring with orange icing, replace 2–4 tablespoons of candied cherries with 3–5 tablespoons golden raisins. Omit the lemon juice and mix 4–5 teaspoons orange juice with the confectioners' sugar.

bûche de noël

Serves **10**

Preparation time **40 minutes**, plus cooling

Cooking time **20 minutes**

3 **eggs**

⅔ cup **confectioners' sugar**, plus extra for dusting

⅓ cup **all-purpose flour**

¼ cup **unsweetened cocoa**

1¼ cups **heavy cream**

⅔ cup canned **sweetened chestnut puree**

7 oz **dark chocolate**, broken into pieces

Grease a 13 x 9 inch jelly pan and line it with nonstick parchment paper. Whisk the eggs and sugar in a heatproof bowl over a pan of hot water until the mixture leaves a trail when the beaters are lifted. Sift in the flour and cocoa and fold in.

Pour into the prepared pan and spread into the corners. Bake in a preheated oven at 350°F for about 15 minutes, until just firm. Invert the cake on to a sheet of nonstick parchment paper dusted with confectioners' sugar. Peel away the paper that lined the pan, then roll the sponge in the fresh paper and let cool.

Whip half the cream until softly peaking, then fold in the chestnut puree. Unroll the sponge and spread the chestnut cream over the top (don't worry if the cake cracks). Roll the cake back into a log shape.

Bring the remainder of the cream almost to the boil. Remove from the heat and stir in the chocolate pieces. Let stand until melted, then stir until smooth. Let cool.

Arrange the cake, seam side down, on a serving plate. Lightly whip the chocolate cream, then spread it over the top and sides of the cake, and mark to look like tree bark. Dust with confectioners' sugar just before serving.

For brandy butter yule log, omit the chestnut filling and instead use 1 cup brandy butter (see page 84) mixed with ⅔ cup crème fraîche (or ⅓ cup sour cream and ⅓ cup whipping cream). Dust with unsweetened cocoa instead of confectioners' sugar. Mix 2 teaspoons arrowroot with 1 tablespoon cold water and add to ⅔ cup warmed mulled wine. Heat the sauce until it is thickened and clear and serve with the yule log.

kids' twelfth night crown

Serves **8**

Preparation time **20 minutes**, plus cooling

Cooking time **20–25 minutes**

¾ cup (1½ sticks) **unsalted butter**, softened

¾ cup **superfine sugar**

1⅓ cups **self-rising flour**

½ teaspoon **baking powder**

3 **eggs**

¼ cup **sugar sprinkles**

1 lb **yellow ready-to-use fondant**

16 **black jelly beans**

1 tube **yellow decoration icing**

9 **clear fruit candies**

Kids' orange buttercream

6 tablespoons **unsalted butter**, softened

1⅔ cups **confectioners' sugar**, sifted

1 teaspoon **orange juice**

2 teaspoons grated **orange zest**

Beat the butter, superfine sugar, self-rising flour, baking powder, and eggs together until smooth. Grease two 7 inch sandwich pans and line the bottoms with greased wax paper. Spoon in the mixture and level the tops. Bake in a preheated oven at 350°F for 20–25 minutes. Turn out the cakes onto a wire rack and let cool.

Beat the butter, sugar, and orange juice for the frosting gradually together until light and fluffy, then stir in the zest. Use some of the frosting to sandwich the cakes. Place on a cake board and spread the butter-cream thinly around the sides and thickly over the top. Sprinkle sugar sprinkles over the top.

Knead the ready-to-use fondant until softened, then roll out on a surface lightly dusted with confectioners' sugar. Trim to a 24 x 3½ inch rectangle. Scallop the top edge, using a plain 2½ inch cookie cutter to cut semicircles out of the fondant. Carefully press the strip of fondant around the edge of the cake.

Knead the trimmings, shape into a 24 inch rope and stick around the bottom of the cake with a little buttercream. Trim the ends, if necessary. Spread the remaining buttercream over the fondant rope to resemble a fur trim. Decorate with the jelly beans. Use plenty of decoration to stick the fruit candies onto the crown.

For kids' lemon crown cake, add the grated zest of 1 large lemon to the sponge ingredients. Omit the orange juice and zest from the buttercream and instead use 1 teaspoon lemon juice and 2 teaspoons grated lemon zest. Otherwise, prepare and bake as above.

gingerbread house

Serves **10**

Preparation time **1 hour**, plus chilling, cooling and setpang

Cooking time **15–20 minutes**

¾ cups **honey**

¼ cups **molasses**

5 tablespoons **unsalted butter**

5 cups **all-purpose flour**

1½ teaspoons **baking soda**

1 tablespoon **ground ginger**

1 **egg**

2 **egg yolks**

To decorate

1 quantity **Royal Icing** (see page 10)

8 oz **ready-to-use fondant**

pink and white marshmallows

selection of small **candies**

confectioners' sugar, for dusting

Heat the honey, molasses, and butter in a pan until the butter melts. Sift the flour, baking soda, and ginger into a bowl. Add the egg and yolks to the melted mixture, then pour over the dry ingredients and mix to a dough. Wrap and chill for 30 minutes.

Roll out the dough on a floured surface and cut out 2 rectangles, 6 x 4½ inches, for the roof. Cut out 2 rectangles, 5½ x 3½ inches, for the sides and 2 squares, 5½ inches, for the ends. Trim each end piece into a triangle point running from the center of the top side to halfway down 2 opposite sides. Cut holes for doors and windows. From the trimmings, make a door and 2 shutters per window.

Place on greased baking sheets. Bake in a preheated oven at 350°F for 10–15 minutes, until coloring around the edges. Transfer to a wire rack to cool.

Spoon royal icing into a pastry bag with a writing tip. Spread more icing over a silver cake board. Secure the walls of the house to the board, gluing sections together with icing. Spread the top edges with icing and secure the roof. Let stand for 2 hours to set.

Spread a little royal icing over the roof sections. Knead and roll out the ready-to-use fondant and cover the roof. Use icing trimmings to shape a chimney and snow drifts around the house. Using royal icing, pipe icicles at the roof edges and attach and decorate the shutters and door.

Decorate with marshmallows and candies. Lightly dust the cottage and board with confectioners' sugar.

christmas stocking

Serves **10**
Preparation time **1 hour**

1 roasting-pan **Madeira Cake**
(see page 10)
14 oz **blue ready-to-use**
fondant
¼ quantity **Royal Icing** (see
page 10)
3 oz **white ready-to-use**
fondant
a few **edible silver balls**
white decorator icing
4 oz **pink ready-to-use**
fondant
selection of **candy canes**

Vanilla frosting
8 tablespoons (1 stick)
unsalted butter, softened
2 cups **confectioners' sugar**
1 tablespoon **milk**
1 teaspoon **vanilla extract**

Beat the butter and sugar together, then add the milk and vanilla extract and mix the vanilla frosting to a spreading consistency.

Cut the cake into a stocking shape about 4½ inches wide at the top of the leg. Cut 3 different-size gifts from the trimmings. Split the cake horizontally and sandwich with buttercream. Spread buttercream very thinly over the top and sides of the cake and over the gifts. Transfer to a cake board or plate.

Reserve 2 oz of the blue fondant and knead the rest on a surface lightly dusted with confectioners' sugar until slightly softened. Roll out and drape over the whole cake. Smooth in place and trim off the excess.

Spread the royal icing over the stocking top, then rough up the surface to resemble fleecy stocking lining.

Knead and roll out the white fondant. Using cookie cutters, cut out crescent moons and star shapes. Stick the shapes and silver balls onto the stocking with dots of decorator icing.

Knead and roll out the pink and reserved blue fondants and use to cover the gifts. Cut ribbons from the trimmings and stick onto the gifts with wripang icing. Place at the stocking top. Add the candy canes to the cake board or plate, placing 1 cane at the stocking top.

For chocolate Christmas stocking, replace ½ cup of the flour in the Madeira cake mixture (see page 10) with unsweetened cocoa. Dissolve 2½ tablespoons unsweetened cocoa in 2 tablespoons boiling water and use in the frosting instead of the milk and vanilla extract.

pistachio nut stollen

Serves **15**

Preparation time **40 minutes**, plus rising

Cooking time **50–60 minutes**

4⅔ cups **bread flour**

1 oz **fresh yeast**, crumbled

1¼ cups lukewarm **milk**

⅓ cup **superfine sugar**

1 **egg**

1 teaspoon **vanilla extract**

grated zest of ½ **lemon**

½ teaspoon **salt**

¾ cup (1½ sticks) **butter**

1 cup **chopped candied peel**

1 cup **pistachio nuts**

1⅓ cups **confectioners' sugar**

1 tablespoon **maraschino liqueur**

4 oz **marzipan**

5 tablespoons melted **butter**, to glaze

Sift 4 cups of the flour into a bowl, reserving a little sifted flour for sprinkling. Make a well, add the yeast and milk, and stir into the flour. Sprinkle with a little flour, cover the bowl, and let stand for 20 minutes.

Add the sugar, egg, vanilla extract, lemon zest, and salt to the yeast and knead to form a dry, firm dough. Cover the bowl and let rise for 10 minutes.

Work the butter together with the remaining flour and the mixed peel. Work this mixture into the dough and leave to rise for an additional 30 minutes.

Work the pistachios, ⅓ cup of the confectioners' sugar, and the maraschino into the marzipan. Roll out to ½ inch thick and cut into ½ inch cubes. Work these quickly into the dough. Shape the dough into 2 balls, then roll into 2 stollen about 12 inches long. Place on a baking sheet lined with greased wax paper. Cover with greased plastic wrap and let rise for 20–30 minutes.

Bake in a preheated oven at 400°F for 50–60 minutes, or until a skewer comes out clean. Brush the warm stollen all over with melted butter and dust with the remaining confectioners' sugar.

For Austrian stollen, steep 1 cup raisins, ¼ cup blanched chopped almonds and ⅓ cup chopped, candied peel in 1 tablespoon rum. Use only ¼ cup superfine sugar and raise the quantity of butter worked in to 1 cup (2 sticks). Omit the candied peel, pistachios, confectioners' sugar, maraschino, and marzipan, and instead work the steeped fruit into the dough. Let rise for 30 minutes and continue as above.

fruit & nut ring

Serves **12**

Preparation time **30 minutes**,
  plus cooling

Cooking time about 1¾ **hours**

1 cup finely chopped **pitted,
  dried prunes**

¾ cup finely chopped **dried
  apricot halves**

6 tablespoons **dark rum**

¾ cup (1½ sticks) **unsalted
  butter**, softened

¾ cup **packed dark brown
  sugar**

3 **eggs**

1 cup **whole-wheat flour**

1 cup **all-purpose flour**

¾ teaspoon **baking powder**

¾ teaspoon **ground allspice**

¼ teaspoon **ground ginger**

1 cup **chopped nuts**

1¼ cups **raisins**

grated zest of 1 **lemon**

grated zest of 1 **orange**

1 tablespoon **molasses**

Topping

about ¼ cup **red-currant jelly**,
  melted

mixed nuts

pitted dried prunes

candied cherries

Grease and line the sides of a 10 inch springform Bundt pan with 2 strips of nonstick parchment paper or greased wax paper.

Soak the prunes and apricots in rum together for about 15 minutes while you are preparing the rest of the ingredients.

Cream the butter and sugar together until pale and very light and fluffy. Beat in the eggs, one at a time, following each with 1 tablespoon whole-wheat flour. Sift the all-purpuse flour with the baking powder and spices and fold in with the remaining whole-wheat flour. Mix in all the other ingredients, including the soaked fruit plus any excess liquid in the bowl.

Turn into the tube pan and level the top. Tie a piece of newspaper, folded into a treble thickness, around the outside of the pan. Bake in a preheated oven at 300°F for about 1¾ hours or until a skewer inserted in the cake comes out clean. Let stand in the pan until cold, then remove carefully and peel off the lining paper.

Brush the cake with the red-currant jelly, then arrange the nuts, prunes, and cherries decoratively on the top. Brush again with more jelly and let set.

For cherry & nut ring, omit the dried apricots and use ⅔ cup finely chopped candied cherries instead. Steep the prunes and cherries in 6 tablespoons cherry brandy instead of rum.

smiling snowman

Serves **12**
Preparation time **1 hour**

2 ovenproof bowl **Madeira Cakes** (see page 10)
½ quantity **Vanilla frosting** (see page 120)
2 tablespoons **smooth apricot jam**
1 large **store-bought muffin**
1½ quantities **Royal Icing** (see page 10)
1 oz **orange ready-to-use fondant**
½ oz **black ready-to-use fondant**
2 oz **red ready-to-use fondant**
1 oz **yellow ready-to-use fondant**
confectioners' sugar, for dusting

Sandwich the cakes with the vanilla frosting to make the snowman's body and stand upright on a cake board or plate. Spread jam thinly all over the outside of the cakes to stick the crumbs in place. Press the muffin onto the body so that its domed part forms the snowman's face. Spread the muffin with the remaining jam.

Cover the cakes completely with royal icing, spreading with a round-bladed knife and pulling it into peaks with the back of the knife.

Knead the ready-to-use fondant on a surface lightly dusted with confectioners' sugar until slightly softened, keeping the colors separate. Shape an orange carrot nose and black pebble eyes, a black mouth, and black buttons. Press onto the snowman. Shape half the red fondant into a round and press on to the snowman's head for a hat. Use a strip of yellow fondant as a hatband.

Shape the rest of the yellow fondant into a rope 7 inches long. Repeat with the remaining orange and red fondant. Twist together, roll out to flatten and trim to a 14 x 1 inch scarf. Make small cuts in either end for a fringe, then wrap around the snowman. Reknead and roll out the trimmings, fringe one side, then roll up and add to the top of the hat for a bobble. Dust with sifted confectioners' sugar for freshly fallen snow.

For lemony snowman, omit the royal icing and instead make up 1 quantity of Vanilla frosting (see page 120), omitpang the milk and adding 2 teaspoons grated lemon zest and 1 tablespoon lemon juice to the mixture. Use to sandwich the cakes and to cover the snowman. Otherwise, prepare as above.

panforte di siena

Serves **15**

Preparation time **20 minutes**, plus cooling

Cooking time **55 minutes**

½ cup **hazelnuts**, toasted, skinned and chopped

½ cup **blanched almonds**, toasted and chopped

⅓ cup chopped **candied orange peel**

⅓ cup chopped **candied lemon peel**

⅓ cup chopped **candied fruit**

2 teaspoons **ground cinnamon**

large pinch of **ground allspice**

⅔ cup **all-purpose flour**

½ cup **honey**

½ cup **superfine sugar**

confectioners' sugar, for dusting

Line a deep sponge pan or a loose-bottom 7–8 inch round cake pan with rice paper. Combine the nuts, peel, and fruit, then sift in the spices and flour and stir until evenly mixed.

Put the honey and superfine sugar into a saucepan and bring slowly to a boil. Pour over the nut mixture and stir well until blended and a sticky mass forms.

Place the mixture in the pan, but don't press down too firmly. Bake in a preheated oven at 300°F for about 50 minutes, or until almost firm to the touch.

Cool in the pan and then remove carefully. If the rice paper is torn or pulled away from the cake, add a new layer, attaching it with a dab of lightly beaten egg white. Dust the top heavily with icing sugar and serve cut into thin wedges.

For chocolate & date panforte, replace 1 tablespoon of the flour with good-quality unsweetened cocoa and replace half the candied orange and lemon peels with ½ cup chopped dates. After dusting the top heavily with confectioners' sugar, sift extra unsweetened cocoa over a simple stencil to make an attractive pattern on top.

tropical christmas cake

Serves **10**

Preparation time **30 minutes**, plus cooling

Cooking time **1¼–1½ hours**

1¼ cups (2½ sticks) **unsalted butter**

1 cup **superfine sugar**

3 extra-large **eggs**, beaten

3½ cups **self-rising flour**

8 oz **canned pineapple rings in syrup**

⅓ cup chopped **candied cherries**

¼ cup chopped **candied peel**

3 tablespoons chopped **angelica**

3 tablespoons chopped **walnuts**

3 tablespoons **dried shredded coconut**

½ cup **golden raisins**

2 tablespoons toasted **coconut shavings**, to decorate

Coconut frosting

3 tablespoons **unsalted butter**

2 cups **confectioners' sugar**

2 tablespoons **dried flaked coconut**

Grease a 9 inch ring mould or 8 inch cake pan and line with nonstick parchment paper or greased wax paper. Cream the butter and sugar until soft and light, then gradually beat in the eggs. Sift the flour and fold into the creamed mixture.

Drain the canned pineapple, setpang aside 1 tablespoon of the syrup for the frosting and 3 tablespoons of the syrup for the cake. Chop the pineapple rings finely. Fold the dried fruit, nuts, and pineapple into the cake mixture with the coconut, golden raisins and the 3 tablespoons of pineapple syrup.

Put the mixture into the ring mold or cake pan. Bake in a preheated oven, 325°F for 1¼ hours if using a ring mold and 1½ hours if using a cake pan. Cool for at least 10 minutes in the pan, then turn out onto a wire rack and let cool completely.

Melt the butter for the frosting in a pan, then remove from the heat. Sift in the confectioners' sugar, then add the remaining pineapple syrup and the coconut. Stir to combine, then spread the frosting over the top of the cake and a little down the sides. Sprinkle with toasted coconut shavings.

For ginger cake, omit the pineapple, cherries, candied peel, angelica, walnuts, coconut, and golden raisins and instead chop 5 pieces of preserved ginger in syrup and stir into the cake mixture with 2 tablespoons of the syrup, 1 teaspoon ground ginger, 1 teaspoon grated fresh ginger, and 2 tablespoons milk. For the frosting, replace the pineapple syrup and coconut with 2 pieces of chopped preserved ginger and the juice of 1 lemon.

small cakes
& cookies

rich mince pies

Makes **12**
Preparation time **20 minutes**
Cooking time **20 minutes**

2 cups **all-purpose flour**
6 tablespoons chilled
   unsalted butter, diced
½ cup **ground almonds**
2 tablespoons **superfine
   sugar**, plus extra for
   sprinkling
grated zest of **1 orange**
1 **egg**, beaten
2–3 tablespoons **orange juice**
1 cup **mincemeat**
a little **milk** or beaten **egg**,
   to glaze

Place the flour in a bowl, add the butter, and rub in with the fingertips until the mixture resembles fine bread crumbs. Stir in the ground almonds, sugar and orange zest, then add the beaten egg and orange juice and mix to a firm dough.

Knead the dough briefly on a lightly floured surface, then roll out thinly and stamp out twelve 3½ inch rounds with a pastry cutter. Line 12 cups in a muffin pan with the pastry, pressing the pastry rounds into the cups. Add 1 teaspoon mincemeat to each shell.

Roll out the remaining pastry and cut into 2 inch rounds to cover the mince pies. Use a small star cutter to cut out stars from half the pastry lids.

Dampen the edges of the shells and press the lids down lightly to seal them. Brush the tops of the pies with a little milk or beaten egg and sprinkle lightly with the sugar.

Bake in a preheated oven at 400°F for 20 minutes, until golden. Let cool slightly in the pans, then transfer to a wire rack to cool completely.

For puff pastry mince pies, thinly roll out 1 lb store-bought puff pastry. Cut into rounds and fill with mincemeat as above. Brush each pie with a little beaten egg or milk and sprinkle with slivered almonds. Bake at the above temperature for 20–25 minutes or until puffed and golden.

christmas stars

Makes **12**
Preparation time **35 minutes**,
  plus cooling
Cooking time **18–20 minutes**

2 oz **white ready-to-use
  fondant**
Orange Frosting (see page
  140)
½ cup **dried flaked coconut**

Cupcakes
10 tablespoons (1¼) **unsalted
  butter**, softened
¾ cup **superfine sugar**
1⅓ cups **self-rising flour**
3 **eggs**
1 teaspoon **vanilla extract**

Line a 12-section cupcake pan with paper liners. Beat all the cake ingredients together until light and creamy. Divide the mixture evenly among the cake liners. Bake in a preheated oven at 350°F for 18–20 minutes, until risen and just firm to the touch. Transfer to a wire rack to cool.

Knead the white ready-to-use fondant on a surface lightly dusted with confectioners' sugar until slightly softened. Roll out thickly and cut out star shapes using a small star-shaped cookie cutter. Transfer to a cookie sheet lined with nonstick parchment paper and let harden while decorating the cakes.

Spread the frosting roughly over the cakes and scatter with coconut. Gently press 2 stars into the top of each cake and let set.

For chocolate Christmas stars, make the cupcakes as above, substituting 2½ tablespoons unsweetened cocoa for 2 tablespoons of the flour. Replace the orange frosting with chocolate butter icing, made by beating together 6 tablespoons softened unsalted butter, 1 cup confectioners' sugar, and 1 tablespoon unsweetened cocoa dissolved in 1 tablespoon boiling water until smooth. Bake and decorate as above.

mini iced gingerbread cakes

Makes **12**
Preparation time **10 minutes**, plus cooling
Cooking time **15–20 minutes**

8 tablespoons (1 stick) **unsalted butter**
1 cup **light corn syrup**
⅓ cup **packed dark brown sugar**
2 cups **self-rising flour**
1 teaspoon **ground ginger**
1 teaspoon **ground allspice**
½ teaspoon **baking soda**
1¼ cups **milk**
2 **eggs**
1 cup **confectioners' sugar**
4 teaspoons **water**
candied cherries, chopped

Line a 12-section muffin pan with large muffin paper liners. Put the butter, syrup, and sugar in a saucepan. Heat gently, stirring with a wooden spoon, until the butter has completely melted.

Take the pan off the heat. Sift the flour, spices, and baking soda into a bowl. Beat the milk and eggs together in a pitcher with a fork. Add the dry ingredients to the pan, mix with a wooden spoon, then gradually beat in the milk mixture until smooth.

Pour the gingerbread mixture into the muffin liners until two-thirds full. Bake in the center of a preheated oven at 350°F for 10–15 minutes until well risen and the tops spring back when pressed with the fingertips. Cool in the pan.

Sift the confectioners' sugar into a bowl. Gradually mix in the measured water to make a smooth, thick icing. Scatter the cherries over the cakes, drizzle with the icing, and let set.

For snow-covered ginger muffins, stir 3 tablespoons chopped candied ginger into the mix before pouring into the liners, then bake as above. To decorate, mix 4 teaspoons water with 1⅔ cups confectioners' sugar, sifted, to make a smooth, spoonable icing. Drizzle lines of icing over the cakes and top with small slices of candied ginger. Let set before serving.

christmas trees

Serves **12**
Preparation time **25 minutes**

1 baking pan **Madeira Cake**
  (see page 10)
green and **silver sugar pearls**
12 **white marshmallows**

Orange Frosting
8 tablespoons (1 stick)
  unsalted butter, softened
2 cups **confectioners' sugar**,
  sifted
grated zest of 1 **orange** and
  1 tablespoon of the juice

Place the butter in a bowl and gradually beat in the confectioners' sugar until light and fluffy. Stir in the orange zest and juice.

Cut the cake horizontally into 3 short strips. Cut each strip into 3 triangles and use the half-triangle left at each end to make a fourth triangle, butting the halves together with a little frosting. Create a total of 12 triangles—9 whole ones and 3 made of butted-together halves.

Spread the tops and sides of the cakes thinly with the frosting to stick the crumbs in place, then spread with a thicker layer of frosting. Arrange the triangles on a cake board or plate.

Place a marshmallow at the bottom of each triangle for a tub. Press on sugar pearls for decorations.

For chocolate Christmas trees, follow the recipe for the Madeira cake (see page 10), substituting ⅓ cup unsweetened cocoa for the same amount of flour and increasing the quantity of baking powder to 1½ teaspoons. Use large chocolates for the tubs. Alternatively, cut a small strip of sponge off the cake before making the triangles, cut the strip into 12 for the tubs, and wrap each one in red ready-to-use fondant.

mini christmas cakes

Makes **12**

Preparation time **30 minutes**, plus cooling

Cooking time **25 minutes**

10 tablespoons (1¼ stick) **unsalted butter**

⅔ cup **packed light brown sugar**

1⅔ cups **self-rising flour**

3 **eggs**

1 teaspoon **almond extract**

⅓ cup **chopped nuts**

⅓ cup **mixed dried fruit**

2 tablespoons **smooth apricot jam**

1⅓ cups **confectioners' sugar**

4–5 teaspoons cold **water**

1 oz **green ready-to-use fondant**

1 oz **red ready-to-use fondant**

Marzipan

1 cup **ground hazelnuts** or **almonds**

¼ cup **superfine sugar**

⅓ cup **confectioners' sugar**

a few drops of **yellow food coloring**

1 tablespoon **egg white**

Line a 12-section cupcake pan with paper cupcake liners. Put the butter, sugar, flour, eggs, and almond extract in a mixing bowl and beat for 1–2 minutes until light and creamy. Add the nuts and dried fruit and stir in until evenly combined. Divide the mixture evenly among the cake liners. Bake in a preheated oven at 350°F for 25 minutes, until risen and just firm to the touch. Transfer to a wire rack to cool.

Put the nuts, sugars, and food coloring for the marzipan in a bowl. Add the egg white and mix with a round-bladed knife until the mixture starts to cling together. Finish mixing the paste by hand until smooth and very firm. Lightly knead and shape into a thick sausage, 3½ inches long. Cut into 12 slices.

Spread ½ teaspoon jam on the center of each cake, then place a marzipan slice on top.

Put the confectioners' sugar in a bowl and add the measured water to make a thick smooth paste—the icing should hold its shape but not feel too firm. Gently spread the icing over the marzipan.

Knead and roll out the green and red ready-to-use fondant and use to make small holly leaves and berries. Press onto the tops of the cakes to decorate.

For snow-dusted Christmas cakes, make the cupcakes as above. Thinly spread smooth apricot jam over the tops, then dust liberally with sifted confectioners' sugar. Top with edible holly leaf decorations made of marzipan or royal icing (see page 10).

reindeer cupcakes

Makes **12**

Preparation time **40 minutes**, plus cooling

Cooking time **13–15 minutes**

1 tablespoon **unsweetend cocoa**

1 tablespoon boiling **water**

8 tablespoons (1 stick) **unsalted butter**, softened

2 **eggs**

⅔ cup **superfine sugar**

1 cup **self-rising flour**

5 oz **dark chocolate**, broken into pieces

6 **candied cherries**, halved

1 small packet **candy-coated chocolate drops**

Frosting

1 tablespoon **unsweetened cocoa**

1 tablespoon boiling **water**

4 tablespoons **unsalted butter**, softened

1 cup **confectioners' sugar**

Line a 12-section cupcake with red foil cake liners. Put the cocoa into a bowl and mix to a smooth paste with the boiling water.

Put the butter, eggs, superfine sugar, and flour into a bowl and beat until smooth. Stir in the cocoa paste, then divide the mixture among the paper cake liners. Bake in a preheated oven at 350°F for 13–15 minutes, until they are well risen and spring back when pressed with a fingertip. Let cool.

Melt the chocolate in a heatproof bowl over a pan of gently simmering water. Spoon most of the melted chocolate (reserve a little and keep warm in the bowl) into a paper pastry bag, snip off the tip and pipe lines of chocolate about 2½ inches long on a baking sheet lined with nonstick parchment paper. Pipe on branches for antlers. Make enough for 2 per cake, with extras in case of breakages.

Make the unsweetened cocoa with the boiling water. Add the butter, then gradually beat in the confectioners' sugar until smooth. Spread over the tops of the cupcakes.

Add to each a cherry half for a nose and 2 chocolate drops for eyes, piping on the remaining melted chocolate to make eyeballs. Peel the set antlers off the parchment paper and stick at angles into the cupcakes.

For Christmas robin cakes, make the cakes as above and spread the chocolate frosting smoothly over the tops. Use melted chocolate to pipe the outline of a robin on each cake. Finish by adding a sliver of candied cherry for the robin's red breast.

baby panettones

Makes **8**

Preparation time **25 minutes**,
  plus rising

Cooking time **20–25 minutes**

2 teaspoons **active dry yeast**

²⁄₃ cup **superfine sugar**, plus
  1 teaspoon

¾ cup hand-hot **milk**

3 tablespoons **bread flour**

4 extra large **eggs**, plus
  2 **yolks**

2 teaspoons **vanilla extract**

finely grated zest of
  2 **lemons**

¾ cup (1½ sticks) **salted
  butter**, very soft and diced

1 cups **mixed dried fruit**

Grease eight 14 fl oz clean food cans and line with wax paper that extends above the rims. Grease the paper. Stir the yeast and 1 teaspoon sugar into the milk in a large, warm bowl, and let stand for 10 minutes or until frothy. Stir in ¾ cup of the flour. Cover with plastic wrap and let stand for 30 minutes.

Add the eggs and yolks, the remaining flour, and the sugar, vanilla extract, lemon zest, and butter. Mix with a round-bladed knife to make a soft dough, adding a little more flour if the dough feels sticky. Turn out onto a lightly floured surface and knead until smooth and elastic. Let stand to rise in a lightly greased bowl, covered with plastic wrap, for 2–4 hours or until doubled in size.

Punch down the dough (punch your fist into the risen dough so that it collapses as the air is excluded) and lightly knead in the dried fruit. Cut the dough into 8 pieces and drop into the cans. Cover and let to rise until the dough almost reaches the rims.

Bake in a preheated oven at 400°F for 20–25 minutes or until risen and golden. Let stand for 5 minutes, then cool on a wire rack.

For whole panettone, shape the mixture into 1 large ball. Place in a 6 inch round cake pan, greased and lined with a double layer of greased wax paper that extends 4 inches above the rim. Cover and let stand to rise. Bake for 15 minutes at 400°F, then reduce to 350°F and bake for 40 minutes, until well risen and an inserted skewer comes out clean. Let stand for 10 minutes, then cool on a wire rack.

marzipan & apple pies

Makes **12**

Preparation time **10–15 minutes**, plus chilling

Cooking time **15–20 minutes**

1 cup **all-purpose flour**

1 cup **whole-wheat flour**

pinch of **salt**

8 tablespoons (1 stick) **unsalted butter**, chilled

3–4 tablespoons **water**

1 large **cooking apple**, peeled, cored, and coarsely chopped

3 oz **marzipan**, cut into (¼ inch) cubes

milk, for brushing

1 tablespoon **raw brown sugar** (optional)

Mix the flours and salt in a bowl, then grate in the butter. Distribute the butter gently through the flour, using a round-bladed knife, then add the measured water and mix to a fairly firm dough. Put the pastry into a plastic bag and chill in the refrigerator for 1 hour, if possible.

Roll out the pastry thinly on a lightly floured surface. Cut out 12 rounds using a 3½ inch fluted cutter and 12 rounds using a 2 inch fluted cutter. Line a 12-section muffin pan with the larger rounds.

Mix the apples and marzipan together in a bowl. Spoon the mixture into the pastry shells, packing it in well.

Brush both sides of the remaining rounds with milk and lay them on top of the tartlets in the pan. Press the edges together to seal and sprinkle each one with a little raw brown sugar, if liked. Bake near the top of a preheated oven at 425°F for 15–20 minutes, until golden brown. Remove carefully from the tins and let cool slightly on a wire rack. Serve warm or cold.

For pear & marzipan pastries, replace the apples with 2 medium pears, peeled, cored, and coarsely chopped. Combine with the marzipan. Thinly roll out 12 oz store-bought puff pastry and cut into six 4 inch squares. Top each one with a spoonful of pear and marzipan filling and fold in half to form triangular parcels. Seal the edges and prick holes in the top. Brush with milk, dredge with superfine sugar, and bake as above for 20 minutes, until risen and golden.

meringue snowmen

Makes **9–12**
Preparation time **20 minutes**
Cooking time **45–60 minutes**

3 **egg whites**
⅔ cup **superfine sugar**
currants
candied cherries, cut into
 pieces
chopped candied peel
 (optional)

Line a baking sheet with nonstick parchment paper. Whisk the egg whites in a large bowl until they form soft peaks. Whisk in the sugar, a teaspoon at a time, until it has all been added and you have a thick, glossy meringue mixture. You should be able to hold the bowl upside down without the mixture falling out.

Use a teaspoon to place a meringue head on a baking sheet, then use a tablespoon for the snowman's body. Repeat to make 9–12 snowmen. Attach currants for their eyes and pieces of candied cherry for their mouths. Give them buttons down their fronts using more currants or pieces of candied peel.

Bake in a preheated oven at 225°F for 45–60 minutes or until the meringues are firm and may be easily peeled off the paper. Let cool on the baking sheet.

For marron meringues, make the meringue mix as above and place in a pastry bag fitted with a large star tip. Pipe 4 inch bars on the lined baking sheet and cook as above. To assemble, beat 1 cup sweetened chestnut puree with 1 tablespoon rum or coffee liqueur until smooth. Whip 1¼ cups heavy cream until stiff and fold through the chestnut mixture. Use the chestnut cream to sandwich the meringues in pairs. Makes 8–10 meringues.

tree decorations

Makes **25**

Preparation time **40 minutes**, plus cooling

Cooking time **15–17 minutes**

6 tablespoons **unsalted butter**
¼ cup **light corn syrup**
½ cup **superfine sugar**
1 teaspoon **ground cinnamon**
½ teaspoon **ground ginger**
large pinch of **ground allspice**
2⅓ cup **all-purpose flour**
1 teaspoon **baking soda**
about 3 tablespoons **milk**
4 oz **white decorator icing**
a few **edible colored balls** (optional)

Put the butter, syrup, and sugar into a saucepan and heat gently, stirring occasionally, until the butter has melted and the sugar dissolved. Take the pan off the heat and stir in the spices. Mix together the flour and baking soda and then beat into the spicy butter mixture, adding enough milk to make a smooth dough.

Turn out the dough onto a board and let stand for 5–10 minutes, until it is cool enough to handle. Knead well, then roll out on a lightly floured surface or a piece of nonstick parchment paper.

Cut out Christmas shapes using star, tree, stocking, bell or any other festive cutters. Reroll the trimmings and cut out more shapes. Transfer the shapes to lightly greased baking sheets.

Make a hole in the top of each biscuit with the end of a skewer or a teaspoon handle and bake in a preheated oven at 350°F for 10–12 minutes, until browned. Enlarge the hole for ribbon if needed. Let cool on the baking sheets.

Pipe the icing onto the cookies, add the colored balls, if using, and let harden. Thread fine ribbons through the holes in the cookies and tie onto the Christmas tree.

For children's tree cookies, make the cookie dough, cut out tree shapes (omitting the holes), and bake as above. When cool, decorate the tree cookies using different colored decorator icing to represent tinsel and mini candy-coated chocolate drops as ball ornaments.

chocolate viennese whirls

Makes **12**
Preparation time **15 minutes**,
  plus cooling
Cooking time **15–20 minutes**

14 tablespons (1¾ sticks)
  unsalted butter, softened
½ cup **superfine sugar**
1⅔ cups **all-purpose flour**
½ teaspoon **baking powder**
¼ cup **unsweetened cocoa**
2 teaspoons **milk**
3½ oz **dark chocolate**, broken
  into pieces

Line a 12-section muffin pan with paper cake liners. Beat together the butter and sugar until pale and creamy. Sift the flour, baking powder, and cocoa powder into the bowl, add the milk, and beat well to make a smooth paste.

Spoon the mixture into a pastry bag fitted with a large star tip and pipe rings into the paper liners, leaving a large hole in the center.

Bake the whirls in a preheated oven at 375°F for 15–20 minutes or until slightly risen. Press a hole in the center of each one. Allow to cool in the pan.

Melt the chocolate in a heatproof bowl over a pan of gently simmering water. Spoon a little chocolate into the center of each Viennese whirl. Let set slightly before serving.

For raspberry Viennese whirls, make the Viennese mixture as above, using ¾ cup confectioners' sugar instead of the superfine sugar and replacing the unsweetened cocoa and milk with 1 teaspoon vanilla extract. Pipe the mixture into cake liners as above, then press a still-frozen raspberry into the center of each cake before baking. Let cool in the pan, then add tiny spoonfuls of seedless raspberry jam instead of the melted chocolate to the center of each cake. Dust lightly with confectioners' sugar and serve.

winter wonderland

Makes **1 winter scene**
Preparation time **about 1½ hours**, plus cooling and setting
Cooking time **15 minutes**

double quantity **Spicy Gingerbread dough**, chilled (see page 158)
½ quantity **Royal Icing** (see page 10)
4 oz **red ready-to-use fondant**
1 oz **black ready-to-use fondant**
confectioners' sugar, for dusting

Roll out the gingerbread dough on a lightly floured surface and cut out shapes using a set of Christmas scene cutters. You'll need 2 sleigh sides, 2 sleigh ends, 2 reindeer bodies and 4 pairs of legs, 1 snowman with base, and 1 tree with base. Place the pieces on large greased baking sheets, spacing them slightly apart.

Bake in a preheated oven at 350°F for 15 minutes or until the dough has risen slightly and is darkening at the edges. Let stand for 5 minutes, then transfer to wire racks to cool.

Put the royal icing in a pastry bag fitted with a plain tip. Knead the red ready-to-use fondant until slightly softened, roll out thinly, and cut out 4 top sections for the sleigh sides, using the same cutter as before. Attach using piped royal icing. Roll out the black fondant and cut out small squares for the reindeers' hooves. Shape and secure small red reindeer noses and a red scarf and black hat for the snowman.

Pipe royal icing decorations on the sleigh, reindeer, snowman, and tree. Let set for at least 1 hour.

Assemble the scene by slotting the pieces together. Place on a board and dust with confectioners' sugar.

For gingerbread snowmen, use a snowman cutter to cut out about 20 snowmen from a single quantity of Spicy gingerbread dough and bake as above. Lightly knead 8 oz white ready-to-use fondant, roll out, and cut 20 more snowmen. Stick the icing snowmen on the cooled cookies using piped royal icing. Add a scarf and hat for each snowman as above and add smiling faces using decorator icing.

stenciled cookies

Makes **10**

Preparation time **25 minutes**, plus chilling and cooling

Cooking time **12 minutes**

Spicy gingerbread

8 tablespoons (1 stick) **unsalted butter**, softened

⅓ cup **packed light brown sugar**

1 **egg**, beaten

⅓ cup **molasses**

3 cups **self-rising flour**

1½ teaspoons **ground ginger**

Frosting

4 tablespoons **unsalted butter**, softened

1 cup **confectioners' sugar**, plus extra for dusting

1 tablespoon **milk** or **cream**

Make the spicy gingerbread by beating the butter and sugar together until creamy. Stir in the egg and molasses. Sift in the flour and ground ginger and stir to form a stiff paste. Turn out the dough onto a lightly floured work surface and knead lightly until smooth. Wrap and chill for at least 30 minutes before using.

Roll out the dough thinly on a lightly floured surface and cut out rounds using a 2½ inch round cookie cutter. Place on greased baking sheets, spaced apart, and reroll the trimmings to make extras. Bake in a preheated oven at 350°F for 12 minutes or until the dough has risen slightly and is darkening at the edges. Transfer to a wire rack to cool.

Beat together the butter and a little of the sugar. Gradually beat in the remaining sugar and the milk or cream until smooth. Use to sandwich the cookies together in pairs.

Make templates of a simple Christmas tree and star from 3 inch circles of paper. Lay a template over a cookie and dust with plenty of confectioners' sugar. Carefully lift off the template, shake off excess sugar, and repeat the decoration on the other cookies.

For spicy gingerbread people, make, chill, and roll out the dough as above. Cut out shapes using gingerbread people cutters. Bake on greased baking sheets in a preheated oven at 350°F for 15 minutes or until the dough has risen slightly and is darkening at the edges. Cool on a wire rack, then decorate using decorator icing, ready-to-use fondant, candy-coated chocolate drops, and other candies.

mulled wine cookies

Makes about **25**
Preparation time **15 minutes**,
  plus cooling
Cooking time **25–30 minutes**

1 cup **raisins**
⅔ cup **dried cranberries**
1¼ cups **red wine**
⅛ cup **redcurrant jelly**
pinch of **chili powder**
1 teaspoon **ground cinnamon**
¼ teaspoon **ground cloves**
⅓ cup chopped **walnuts**
⅓ cup chopped **blanched almonds**
3½ oz **dark chocolate**, finely chopped
⅔ cup **self-rising flour**
finely grated zest of **1 orange**
4 tablespoons **unsalted butter**, melted
1 **egg**
confectioners' sugar, for dusting

Put the raisins and cranberries in a small heavy saucepan with the wine, red-currant jelly, and spices. Heat until the jelly dissolves, then bring to the boil and boil for 2–3 minutes, until the syrup is reduced by about half. Let cool.

Mix the nuts and chocolate in a bowl with the flour, orange zest, butter, egg, and fruit mixture to make a paste. Place teaspoons of the mixture, spaced slightly apart, on a lightly greased baking sheet.

Bake the cookies in a preheated oven at 350°F for about 20 minutes until they have spread slightly. Let them on the baking sheet for 3 minutes, then transfer to a wire rack to cool. Dust generously with confectioners' sugar.

For port & cherry cookies, omit the dried cranberries and the red wine and use ½ cup dried cherries and 1¼ cups inexpensive port instead. Replace the blanched almonds with ⅓ cup chopped hazelnuts and continue as above.

triple chocolate biscotti

Makes **about 28**
Preparation time **35 minutes**,
  plus cooling
Cooking time **45 minutes**

4 tablespoons **lightly salted
  butter**, softened
¼ cup **superfine sugar**
1⅓ cups **self-rising flour**
1 teaspoon **baking powder**
½ teaspoon **ground coriander**
finely grated zest of 1 **orange**,
  plus 1 tablespoon of the juice
¼ cup **polenta**
1 **egg**, lightly beaten
¾ cup roughly chopped
  unblanched almonds,
⅓ cup **milk chocolate chips**
5 oz **plain dark chocolate**,
  broken into pieces
2 oz **white chocolate**, broken
  into pieces

Beat the butter and sugar until creamy. Add the flour, baking powder, coriander, orange zest and juice, cornmeal, and egg and mix to form a firm dough. Knead in the almonds. Turn out the dough on a lightly floured surface and gently work in the chocolate chips. Divide the mixture in half and shape each piece into a log about 9 inches long.

Place on a greased baking sheet, spaced well apart, and flatten slightly. Bake in a preheated oven at 325°F for 30 minutes or until risen and just firm. Remove from the oven and let cool on the baking sheet for 15 minutes. Transfer to a board and, using a serrated knife, cut into ½ inch thick slices.

Arrange on the baking sheet, cut sides down, and bake for 15 minutes, until crisp. Transfer to a wire rack and let cool.

Melt the dark and white chocolates in 2 separate heatproof bowls over pans of simmering water. Line a clean baking sheet with nonstick parchment paper. Dip about one-third of each cookie in the dark chocolate, letting the excess fall back into the bowl. Place each cookie on the parchment paper.

Drizzle thin lines of melted white chocolate over the plain dark chocolate to decorate. Let stand in a cool place to set for about 1 hour.

For chocolate & walnut biscotti, omit the ground coriander and almonds and instead use 1 teaspoon vanilla extract and 1 cup chopped walnut pieces. Replace the milk chocolate chips with white chocolate chips and continue as above.

candy cane cookies

Makes **28–30**
Preparation time **50 minutes**, plus cooling
Cooking time **15 minutes**

1 quantity **Vanilla Cookies dough**, chilled (see page 168)
½ quantity **Royal Icing** (see page 10)

First make the candy cane template. On paper draw a walking cane, ½ inch wide and 4 inches long, with a curved end, then cut it out. Roll out the cookie dough on a lightly floured surface. Lay the template over the dough and cut around it about 25 times using a small, sharp knife or scalpel.

Space the shapes slightly apart on greased cookie sheets. Reroll the trimmings to make extras. Bake in a preheated oven at 350°F for 15 minutes or until pale golden. Transfer to a wire rack to cool.

Put the royal icing in a pastry bag fitted with a plain tip and pipe a zigzag line of icing along each cookie. Let the cookies stand in a cool place to set for at least 1 hour before serving.

For Christmas ball decorations, cut the dough into twenty 3¼ inch rounds. Use a skewer to make a small hole ½ inch in from the edge of each circle. Bake as above, repiercing the holes as soon as the cookies come out of the oven. When cool, brush the cookies with smooth apricot jam and sprinkle over bands of green and red sugar sprinkles. Pipe royal icing between the sugar sprinkles and around the edges. Let set for at least 1 hour before threading with thin ribbon.

hazelnut meringues

Makes **25**
Preparation time **20 minutes**
Cooking time **45–60 minutes**

⅔ cup **hazelnuts**
4 **egg whites**
1 cup **superfine sugar**
½ teaspoon **white wine vinegar**
¼ teaspoon **vanilla extract**
½ cup **crème fraîche** (or
 ¼ cup sour cream mixed
 with ¼ cup whipping cream)
1½ cups **red-currants**

Line a baking sheet with nonstick baking paper. Coarsely gzest the hazelnuts in a food processor (or chop them and then crush with a pestle and mortar), then set them aside.

Whisk the egg whites in a large bowl until they form soft peaks. Gradually add the sugar, a teaspoon at a time, whisking until the mixture is very stiff and shiny. The mixture should stay put, even when the bowl is tilted. Fold in the vinegar and vanilla extract, then fold in the ground nuts.

Spoon the meringue mixture onto the lined cookie sheet, to make approximately 25 mini meringues, spacing them apart as they will expand slightly in the oven. Bake in a preheated oven at 225°F for 45–60 minutes or until the meringues are firm and may be easily peeled off the paper.

Let cool on the cookie sheet. Serve the cooled meringues topped with a little crème fraîche and a small sprig of red-currants.

For rose water, cinnamon & orange meringues, replace the hazelnuts with the finely grated zest of 1 orange and replace the vanilla extract with 3 drops rose water and a large pinch of ground cinnamon. Fold in with the vinegar, as above.

falling snowflakes

Makes **14**

Preparation time **50 minutes**, plus chilling and cooling

Cooking time **15 minutes**

½ quantity **Royal Icing** (see page 10)

Vanilla cookies

2 cups **all-purpose flour**

1 cup (2 sticks) chilled **unsalted butter**, diced

1 cup **confectioners' sugar**

2 **egg yolks**

2 teaspoons **vanilla extract**

Citrus glaze

8 teaspoons **lemon**, **lime** or **orange juice**

2 cups **confectioners' sugar**

Combine the flour and butter until the mix resembles fine bread crumbs. Add the sugar, egg yolks, and vanilla extract and mix to a smooth dough. Wrap and chill for at least 30 minutes before using.

Roll out the dough on a lightly floured surface and cut out star shapes, using a 14 inch star cookie cutter. Space them slightly apart on greased cookie sheets, then reroll the trimmings to make extras. Using a skewer make a small hole on each star, near the tip of a point. Bake in a preheated oven at 350°F for 15 minutes or until pale golden. Remove from the oven and immediately remake the holes. Transfer to a wire rack to cool.

Place the citrus juice in a small bowl and gradually beat in the sugar until the glaze thickly coats the back of the spoon. Spread it over the cookies almost to the edges of each star.

Put the royal icing in a pastry bag fitted with a plain tip. Pipe 3 lines across each cookie, then pipe a row of tiny chevrons over each line to create a snowflake effect. Let stand in a cool place to set for at least 1 hour before threading with thin ribbon.

For iced snowflakes, make and cook the cookies as above but omit the hole-making step. Omit the citrus glaze. Lightly knead and roll out 8 oz white ready-to-use fondant. Use the cookie cutter to make star shapes from the fondant and stick to the cookies using a little royal icing. Pipe the lines and chevrons on top of the snowflakes as above.

gingerbread night-lights

Makes **4**

Preparation time **50 minutes**,
 plus cooling

Cooking time **13–15 minutes**

1 quantity **Spicy Gingerbread
 dough**, chilled (see page
 158)

6 oz **colored boiled candies**,
 lightly crushed

½ quantity **Royal Icing** (see
 page 10)

Roll out half the gingerbread dough thinly on a lightly
floured surface and cut out a neat 14 x 7 inch
rectangle. Carefully lift onto a cookie sheet lined with
nonstick parchment paper and trim the edges of the
rectangle. Using a ruler, cut the dough into 8 exact
3¾ in squares. Using a 3¼ inch star cutter, remove a
star shape from each square (cook the stars separately
if desired). Repeat with the second batch of dough on
a second cookie sheet.

Bake the squares in a preheated oven at 350°F for
5 minutes. Remove from the oven and scatter the
crushed candies into the cut-out star areas. Return
to the oven for an additional 8–10 minutes until the
gingerbread is lightly colored and the candies have
melted to fill the stars. (If they haven't completely
spread into the corners, use a toothpick to spread
the syrup while it is still soft.) Recut the edges of the
gingerbread squares to neaten them, then let them
stand on the baking sheets to cool.

Put the royal icing in a pastry bag fitted with a plain
tip. Pipe a line of icing along an inside edge of
4 of the cookies and press together to make 4 sides
of a box shape. Make 3 more box shapes in the
same way. Use the remaining icing in the bag to pipe
decorative lines around the edges of the boxes. Let
stand in a cool place to set for at least 2 hours.

Place a night-light on a small mat or coaster, light it,
and lower a gingerbread box over the top.

edible gifts

mincemeat

Makes 6½ **lb**

Preparation time **20–30 minutes,** plus standing

3⅓ cups chopped dried **currants**

3½ cups chopped **golden raisins**

3½ cups chopped **seedless raisins**

2¾ cups **chopped candied peel**

1 cup finely chopped **blanched almonds**

2 large (about 1 lb) **cooking apples,** peeled, cored, and coarsely grated

2¼ cups **packed dark brown sugar**

1¼ cups chopped **lard**

1 teaspoon **ground nutmeg** or grated **nutmeg**

1 teaspoon **ground cinnamon**

1 teaspoon **ground allspice**

grated zest of 2 **lemons**

juice of 1 **lemon**

2–4 tablespoons **brandy**

Put the currants, golden raisins, raisins, peel, and almonds into a large bowl. Add the apples, sugar, lard, spices, and lemon zest and juice and stir to mix thoroughly.

Cover the bowl with plastic wrap and let the mincemeat stand for 2 days.

Stir the mincemeat again very thoroughly, pouring off any excess liquid. Stir in the brandy.

Pack the mincemeat into warm, dry, sterilized jars (see page 9). Cover each jar with a disk of wax paper, waxed side down, then let stand until cold. Top the jars with cellophane covers or airtight lids. Label and store in a cool, dry place for at least 2 weeks before using. It will keep, unopened, for up to 6 months.

For cranberry mincemeat, use 2⅓ cups each dried currants, golden raisins, and seedless raisins and make up the quantity with 2½ cups dried cranberries. Continue with the recipe as above.

ginger marmalade

Makes **5 lb**
Preparation time **30 minutes**,
 plus standing
Cooking time **2¾ hours**

8 **lemons**
2 large **oranges**
10½ cups **water**
3 inch piece **fresh ginger**,
 sliced and finely shredded
7½ cups **sugar**

Pare the zest thinly from the fruits and cut into fine shreds. Halve the fruits and squeeze out the juice, then put the juice and zest into a large pan with the measured water and ginger.

Chop the fruit halves, including the pith, and tie the pieces in a cheesecloth bag. Add this to the pan and slowly bring the mixture to a boil. Reduce the heat, cover the pan, and simmer for 2 hours or until the ginger and zest are completely tender. Take the pan off the heat and let stand until the cheesecloth is cool enough to handle, then squeeze all the juices back into the marmalade and discard the bag.

Add the sugar to the pan and cook over a low heat, stirring continuously, until the sugar has dissolved. Increase the heat and bring to a boil, then boil rapidly to setting point. Using a slotted spoon, carefully skim off any scum, then let the marmalade stand for 15 minutes to let the fruit settle.

Stir well, then transfer to warm, dry, sterilized jars (see page 9). Cover each jar with a disk of wax paper, waxed side down, then let stand until cold. Top with cellophane covers or airtight lids. Label and store in a cool, dark place. It will keep, unopened, for 3–4 months.

For lime marmalade, wash and dry 6 limes and 2 lemons. Cut into quarters lengthwise and then into long, very fine slices, removing all the seeds. Mix the fruit in a large pan. Add 6¼ cups water, bring to a boil, then reduce the heat, cover, and simmer for 1½ hours. Add 7½ cups sugar and proceed as above.

lime & passion fruit curd

Makes **2 lb**
Preparation time **15 minutes**
Cooking time **30–40 minutes**

1¼ cups **superfine sugar**
finely grated zest and juice of
  4 **limes**
8 tablespoons (1 stick)
  unsalted butter, cut into
  pieces
4 **eggs,** beaten
3 **passion fruits**

Pour a little water into a pan and bring to a boil. Stand a large heatproof bowl over the top, making sure that the bottom of the bowl is not touching the water. Put the sugar and lime zest in the bowl and press them against the edge of the bowl with a wooden spoon to release the oils from the zest.

Pour the lime juice into the bowl through a strainer and add the butter. Heat, stirring occasionally, until the butter has melted. Strain the eggs into the mixture and stir until well mixed. Continue heating gently for 20–30 minutes, stirring occasionally, until very thick. Take the bowl off the pan.

Halve the passion fruits, then scoop out the seeds into the lime curd using a teaspoon. Mix together gently.

Transfer to warm, dry, sterilized jars (see page 9). Cover each jar with a disk of wax paper, placed waxed side down. Let cool, then cover the jars with cellophane covers or airtight lids. The curd will keep in the refrigerator for up to 1 month.

For lemon curd, omit the limes and use 2½ lemons instead. Continue with the recipe as above, omitting the passion fruits.

For mixed citrus curd, use 1 lemon, 1 orange, and 1 lime instead of the 4 limes. Continue as above, omitting the passion fruits.

peach & date chutney

Makes **3–4½ lb**
Preparation time **10 minutes**
Cooking time **50 minutes**

12 **peaches**
3 medium (about 1 lb) **onions**
2 **garlic cloves**, crushed
2 tablespoons grated **fresh ginger**
¾ cup chopped **pitted dates**
1¼ cups **raw brown sugar**
1¼ cups **red wine vinegar**
salt and **black pepper**

Place the peaches in a large bowl, cover with boiling water, and let stand for about 1 minute, then drain and peel them. Halve and pit the peaches and cut the flesh into thick slices.

Put the onions in a pan with the peach slices, garlic, ginger, dates, sugar, and vinegar. Add a generous sprinkling of salt and black pepper and bring the mixture to a boil, stirring continuously, until the sugar has completely dissolved.

Reduce the heat, cover the saucepan, and simmer, stirring frequently, for 45 minutes, until the chutney has thickened.

Transfer the chutney to warm, dry, sterilized jars (see page 9). Cover the surface of each with a disk of wax paper, waxed side down. When cool, seal with an airtight lid. Label the jars and let stand to mature in a cool, dark place for 2 weeks before using. It will keep, unopened, for 6–12 months.

For apricot & date chutney, omit the 12 peaches and use 4½ lb apricots instead. Continue with the recipe as above.

tomato & pepper relish

Makes 4½ **lb**
Preparation time **20 minutes**
Cooking time **35 minutes**

6 medium (about 2 lb) ripe
  tomatoes, skinned and
  chopped
5 large (about 2 lb) **red
  peppers**, cored, seeded,
  and finely chopped
3 medium (about 1 lb) **onions**,
  finely chopped
2 **red chilies**, seeded and
  finely chopped
2 cups **red wine vinegar**
¾ cup **packed light brown
  sugar**
¼ cup **mustard seeds**
2 tablespoons **celery seeds**
1 tablespoon **paprika**
2 teaspoons **salt**
2 teaspoons **black pepper**

Combine all the ingredients in a large saucepan. Bring
the mixture to the boil over a moderate heat, then
reduce the heat and simmer, uncovered, for about
30 minutes, until most of the liquid has evaporated and
the relish has a thick, pulpy consistency. Stir frequently
as the relish thickens.

Transfer the relish to 3 warm, dry, sterilized 1 lb jar
(see page 9). Cover the surface of each with a disk of
wax paper, waxed side down. When cool, seal with an
airtight lid. Label the jars and store in a cool, dry place.
The relish will keep, unopened, for up to 3 months.

For beet & apple relish, put 2 large cooking apples,
peeled, cored, and grated, and 10 medium (about
1 lb) grated raw beet in a large pan with 2 medium
finely chopped onions, 1 tablespoon finely chopped
fresh root ginger, 2 crushed large garlic cloves,
1 teaspoon paprika, 1 teaspoon ground turmeric,
1 cinnamon stick, 2¼ cups packed dark brown sugar
and 2 cups red wine vinegar. Bring to a boil, reduce
the heat, and cover. Simmer, stirring occasionally, for
about 1½ hours, until the relish has thickened and the
beet is tender. Can, cool, and seal as above and let
stand to mature in a cool, dark place for 1 week. (It
will keep, unopened, for 6–9 months.)

blueberries in kirsch

Makes **1 lb**

Preparation time **10 minutes**, plus standing

2½ cups **blueberries**, stalks removed, very soft ones discarded

1 cup **superfine sugar**

1 cup **kirsch**

Prick each blueberry with a fork, then layer the blueberries in a clean, dry jar, sprinkling each layer with some of the sugar.

Pour the kirsch over the sugared blueberries. Seal tightly and shake once or twice.

Let stand in a cool place and turn the jar upside down every day for 4 days until the sugar has completely dissolved. Label the jar and let stand to mature in a cool, dark place for 3–4 weeks before using. The blueberries will keep, unopened, for 6–12 months.

For cherries in kirsch, omit the blueberries and use 2½ cups fresh red or black pitted cherries instead. Continue as above.

spiced sloe gin

Makes **3 cups**
Preparation time **15 minutes**,
  plus standing

4 **sloe plums**, stalks removed
  and soft ones discarded
1 cup **superfine sugar**
3 whole **cloves**
pared zest of 1 **orange**
1 **cinnamon stick**, halved
about 3 cups inexpensive **gin**

Prick each sloe with a fork and drop them into a clean, dry 1 quart wide-necked, screw-topped bottle.

Using a plastic funnel or a cone of paper, pour the sugar into the bottle. Stick the cloves into the orange zest and add to the bottle along with the halved cinnamon stick.

Pour in the gin, seal with an airtight top, and turn the bottle upside down 2–3 times.

Stand the bottle in a cool place and turn it once a day for 7 days until the sugar has completely dissolved.

Label the bottle and let stand to mature in a cool, dark place for 6 months or longer, if you can (the longer you let it stand, the mellower and more delicious it will be). The sloes should be discarded before the gin is served.

For damson gin, omit the sloes and spices and use 4 damson plums instead. Continue as above. (It tastes deliciously boozy spooned on to ice cream.)

For damson vodka, omit the sloes, spices, and gin and use 4 damson plums and about 3 cups vodka instead. Continue as above.

fruit & nut disks

Makes **18**
Preparation time **10 minutes**,
  plus setting
Cooking time **5 minutes**

3½ oz **dark chocolate**,
  broken up
3½ oz **milk chocolate**,
  broken up
3½ oz **white chocolate**,
  broken up
¾ cup **mixed dried tropical
  fruits** (such as pineapple,
  mango, papaya, melon)
3 tablespoons **blanched
  almonds**
3 tablespoons **unblanched
  hazelnuts**

Melt the 3 chocolates in 3 separate heatproof bowls, each over a pan of gently simmering water. Spoon onto 3 separate sheets of nonstick baking paper and spread to 6½ x 5 inch rectangles.

Use a 2 inch round metal cookie cutter to make 6 impressions in each chocolate rectangle to mark the edges of each disk.

Cut the dried fruits into small, flattish pieces and arrange them within the marked disks along with the nuts. Chill or let stand in a cool place until the chocolate is set but not brittle.

Use the cutter to cut out the discs and carefully lift them from the paper. They will keep, in an airtight container in a cool place, for up to 1 month.

For berry & chocolate hearts, melt 7 oz dark chocolate as above. Using an ice-cube tray with heart-shaped molds, spoon in enough melted chocolate to fill 8 of the holes halfway. Sprinkle over ½ cup mixed dried cranberries and blueberries, then fill up with the remaining chocolate. Chill in the refrigerator for at least 1 hour before upturning the ice-cube tray to pop out the chocolates.

creamy pistachio toffee

Makes **30**
Preparation time **15 minutes**,
  plus setting
Cooking time **20 minutes**

1½ cups **granulated sugar**
1¼ cups **heavy cream**
2 tablespoons **unsalted
  butter**
½ cup roughly chopped
  pistachio nuts

Put the sugar and cream in a heavy saucepan and heat gently, stirring occasionally, until the sugar has completely dissolved. Stir the butter into the sugar and cream mixture, insert a sugar thermometer if you have one, and increase the heat. Cook for about 15 minutes until the temperature reaches 250°F or a little of the toffee forms a hard ball when dropped into a bowl of cold water. Stir occasionally at first, then more frequently as the mixture begins to color, froth, and thicken. When the butter begins to separate from the toffee, it is almost ready. Cook for a few more minutes until it changes to a smooth, glossy toffee.

Remove from the heat, quickly stir in the pistachio nuts, then pour the toffee into a greased 7 inch shallow square cake pan. Let cool for 5 minutes, then mark into strips and let cool completely.

Loosen the edges of the toffee from the sides of the pan and turn it out. Break into pieces with a toffee hammer or by hitting a cook's knife with a rolling pin. The toffee will keep, in an airtight container in a cool place, for up to 1 week.

For brazil nut & raisin toffee, replace the chopped pistachios with ⅓ cup roughly chopped brazil nuts and 3 tablespoons raisins. Otherwise proceed as above.

mint & chocolate fudge

Makes **1 lb 12 oz**
Preparation time **15 minutes**,
  plus setting
Cooking time **5 minutes**

7 **strong peppermints**
1 lb **dark chocolate**, chopped
1¼ cups can **sweetened
  condensed milk**
2 oz **milk chocolate** or **white
  chocolate**, melted

Place the peppermints in a plastic bag and crush them with a rolling pin, breaking them into small pieces. Continue to roll and flatten the mints until they are ground to a powder. Line a shallow 7 inch baking pan with nonstick parchment paper.

Put the dark chocolate and condensed milk in a heatproof bowl over a pan of gently simmering water. Let stand until melted, stirring frequently. When melted, stir in the ground peppermints.

Beat the mixture until the ingredients are combined then turn it into the pan, spreading it into the corners. Level the surface and let stand to cool. Chill in the refrigerator for at least 2 hours.

Lift the fudge out of the tin and peel off the paper. Melt the milk or white chocolate in a heatproof bowl over a pan of gently simmering water, then place in a paper pastry bag. Snip off the tip and scribble lines of chocolate over the fudge. When the chocolate is set, cut the fudge into ¾ inch squares. It will keep for up to 2 weeks in the refrigerator.

For coffee & orange chocolate fudge, omit the peppermints and instead add the finely grated zest of 1 small orange and 1 teaspoon instant espresso powder to the melted chocolate and condensed milk mixture. Continue as above.

chocolate & pine nut praline

Makes 7½ oz
Preparation time **15 minutes**,
  plus setting
Cooking time **10 minutes**

⅓ cup **pine nuts**
¼ cup **slivered almonds**
1 cup **superfine sugar**
⅓ cup **water**
2 oz **dark chocolate**, broken
  into pieces

Lightly toast the pine nuts and almonds. Break up the nuts in a food processor or use a mortar and pestle until the nuts are broken into slightly smaller pieces, but not too finely ground.

Put the sugar and measured water in a small heavy saucepan and heat very gently, stirring until the sugar dissolves. Bring to a boil and cook, without stirring, until the syrup turns to golden caramel. This will take 6–8 minutes. Immediately dip the bottom of the pan in cold water to prevent further cooking (if you overcook it, the resulting praline will taste bitter) and stir in the nuts.

Work quickly as you turn the praline onto a large lightly greased baking sheet, spreading it out in a thin layer before it starts to set. Let stand for about 1 hour, until the praline is brittle.

Melt the chocolate in a heatproof bowl over a pan of gently simmering water. Break the praline into pieces and place on a wire rack. Drizzle with the melted chocolate, then let stand to set. The praline will keep, in an airtight container in a cool place, for up to 1 week.

For chocolate & macadamia nut praline, toast ⅓ cup unsalted macadamia nuts and 3 tablespoons chopped hazelnuts and use instead of the pine nuts and slivered almonds. Instead of drizzling melted dark chocolate over the praline, coat the pieces in 2 oz melted milk chocolate and let set.

rocky road clusters

Makes **28**
Preparation time **40 minutes**,
  plus setting
Cooking time **10 minutes**

1 cup **mixed whole nuts**
  (such as cashews, hazelnuts,
  pistachios)
10 oz **dark chocolate**, broken
  into pieces
1 tablespoon **unsalted butter**
2 tablespoons **confectioners'
  sugar**
2 tablespoons **heavy cream**

Put the nuts on a piece of aluminium foil on a baking sheet, then toast under a preheated hot broiler for 3–4 minutes, until golden. Let cool slightly, then chop roughly.

Melt 3 oz of the chocolate in a heatproof bowl over a pan of gently simmering water. Stir the butter, sugar, and cream into the melted chocolate until smooth and glossy, then mix in all but 2 tablespoons of the chopped nuts.

Drop teaspoons of the mixture onto a baking sheet lined with nonstick parchment paper. Chill for 2–3 hours until the mixture is firm.

Melt the remaining chocolate as before. Coat the nut clusters in the melted chocolate by holding them on a fork, one at a time, over the bowl of chocolate and spooning some of it over the top with a teaspoon. When the excess chocolate has dripped away, return the cluster to the paper-lined sheet and repeat with the remainder.

Put the chocolates in a cool place and let set for at least 1 hour, then sprinkle with the reserved nuts. They will keep in the refrigerator for up to 4 days.

For white chocolate clusters, reduce the quantity of mixed whole nuts to ¾ cup. Melt 3 oz white chocolate instead of the dark chocolate and stir in the butter, sugar, cream, and nuts as above. Drop spoonfuls of the mixture onto a baking sheet, chill, and dust with 2 tablespoons sifted confectioners' sugar to finish.

white chocolate mint truffles

Makes **20**
Preparation time **30 minutes**,
  plus cooling and setting
Cooking time **4–5 minutes**

½ cup **heavy cream**
5 oz **white chocolate**, broken
  into pieces
5 **strong, hard, white
  peppermints**
⅓ cup **confectioners' sugar**

Pour the cream into a heavy saucepan and add the chocolate. Heat gently, stirring occasionally, for about 4–5 minutes, until the chocolate has melted. Let cool.

Whisk the cream mixture until thick, then chill in the refrigerator for 3–4 hours.

Put the peppermints into a plastic bag, crush them with a rolling pin, then stir into the chilled cream mixture. Drop teaspoons of the soft mixture onto a plate and chill for 1 hour or freeze for 30 minutes until firm.

Sprinkle the confectioners' sugar on to another plate, then roll the truffles in the sugar to form neat balls. When packed in the gift box, dust with the remaining sugar. Chill for at least 2 hours before using. The truffles will keep in the refrigerator for up to 4 days.

For chocolate rum truffles, melt 3 oz dark chocolate in a heatproof bowl over a pan of simmering water. Remove from the heat. Beat 2 tablespoons unsalted butter and 1 cup confectioners' sugar, sifted, together until light and fluffy. Mix in the cooled, melted chocolate and 2 tablespoons dark rum. Chill until firm, then shape into 1 inch balls and roll each ball in unsweetened cocoa. Makes about 16 truffles that will keep in the refrigerator for 2–3 weeks.

caramelized pecans

Makes **35**
Preparation time **40 minutes**
Cooking time **20 minutes**

⅓ cup **blanched hazelnuts**
2 teaspoons **powdered egg white**
¼ cup **superfine sugar**
1¾ cups **pecans**
1 cups **granulated sugar**
⅓ cup **water**

Place the hazelnuts on a baking sheet and broil under a preheated broiler until lightly browned. Let cool slightly, then gzest finely in a food processor or blender or crush using a mortar and pestle.

Reconstitute the egg white with 2 tablespoons warm water, according to the package instructions, then add the superfine sugar and ground hazelnuts and mix to a stiff marzipan paste. Sandwich the pecans together in pairs with a little of the hazelnut marzipan.

Put the granulated sugar and measured water in a heavy saucepan and heat gently, without stirring, until the sugar has completely dissolved. Increase the heat and cook for 10–15 minutes, until the syrup has turned golden.

Plunge the bottom of the pan into a bowl of cold water to prevent the syrup from cooking and darkening further. Drop the sandwiched pecans, one at a time, into the caramel. Lift out with a fork and let stand on a greased baking sheet to cool and harden. They will keep, in an airtight container in a cool place, for up to 4 days.

For marzipan walnuts, use 1 cup walnut halves instead of the pecans. Omit the caramel glazing and instead sandwich the walnut halves together with a little of the hazelnut marzipan.

cranberry blondies

Makes **20**
Preparation time **25 minutes**
Cooking time **30–35 minutes**

7 oz **white chocolate**, broken
  into pieces
8 tablespoons (1 stick)
  unsalted butter
3 **eggs**
¾ cups plus 2 tablespoons
  superfine sugar
1 teaspoon **vanilla extract**
1¼ cups **all-purpose flour**
1 teaspoon **baking powder**
⅔ cup **dried cranberries**

Line a 7 x 11 x 2 inch baking tin with nonstick parchment paper and snip diagonally into the corners so that the paper fits snugly.

Melt half the chocolate and the butter in a heatproof bowl over a pan of gently simmering water. Whisk the eggs, sugar, and vanilla extract in a separate bowl with an electric mixer until light and frothy and the beaters leave a trail when lifted.

Fold the chocolate and butter mixture into the beaten eggs with a metal spoon. Sift the flour and baking powder over the top and then fold in gently. Chop the remaining chocolate and fold half of it into the mixture with half the cranberries.

Pour the mixture into the pan and sprinkle with the remaining chocolate and cranberries. Bake in a preheated oven at 350°F for 30–35 minutes until well risen. Let cool in the pan.

Lift out of the pan, peel off the paper, and cut the cake into squares. The blondies will keep, in an airtight container in a cool place, for a few days.

For rum & raisin chocolate brownies, use 7 oz dark chocolate in place of the white chocolate and omit the vanilla extract. Replace the cranberries with ½ cup raisins, soaked overnight in 3 tablespoons rum. If liked, drizzle the cake with melted milk chocolate before cutting into squares.

quick hazelnut melts

Makes **20**
Preparation time **10 minutes**
Cooking time **15 minutes**

⅓ cup **blanched hazelnuts**
8 tablespoons (1 stick)
   unsalted butter, softened
¼ cup **superfine sugar**
1¼ cups **all-purpose flour**

Gzest the hazelnuts in a food processor or blender, or crush using a mortar and pestle, until fairly smooth but still retaining a little texture. Brown in a heavy skillet over a low heat until evenly golden. Pour into a bowl and stir until cool.

Beat the butter and sugar together until the mixture is creamy. Add the flour and cooled nuts and mix well to form a soft dough.

Shape walnut-size pieces of dough into balls, then pat into flat ovals. Place on a greased baking sheet and flatten slightly with a fork.

Bake in a preheated oven at 375°F for 12 minutes, until just golden. Cool on a wire rack. They will keep, in an airtight container in a cool place, for a few days.

For almond hearts, beat 1 cup (2 sticks) softened butter with 1 cup confectioners' sugar, sifted, and 1 egg yolk until pale and creamy. Add 1⅓ cups ground almonds and 3 cups all-purpose flour, sifted, and knead to a firm dough. Shape into a ball, wrap in plastic wrap, and refrigerate for 2 hours. Roll out to ¼ inch thick and use a heart-shaped cutter to make 40 hearts. Place on a baking sheet, brush with beaten yolk, and top each heart with a blanched almond half. Bake at 400°F for 10–12 minutes. Cool on the baking sheet for 5 minutes, then transfer to a wire rack.

chocolate ring cookies

Makes **16**
Preparation time **40 minutes**,
  plus chilling and cooling
Cooking time **15 minutes**

2 cups **all-purpose flour**
¼ cup **cocoa powder**
1 cup (2 sticks) chilled
  unsalted butter, diced
1 cup plus 2 tablespoons
  confectioners' sugar
2 **egg yolks**
2 teaspoons **vanilla extract**
4 oz **white chocolate**, broken
  into pieces
3 oz **plain dark chocolate**, in
  a block
½ cup roughly chopped
  unblanched hazelnuts,
candied rose petals

Put the flour, cocoa, and butter in a bowl and rub in with the fingertips until the mixture resembles fine bread crumbs. Add the sugar, egg yolks and vanilla extract and mix to a smooth dough. Wrap and chill for at least 30 minutes before using.

Roll out the dough on a lightly floured surface, then cut out rounds using an 3¾ inch round cookie cutter. Use a 1¼ inch round cutter to cut out the centers to make rings. Place on greased baking sheets, spaced slightly apart, and reroll the trimmings to make extras. Bake in a preheated oven at 350°F for 15 minutes or until beginning to darken around the edges. Cool on a wire rack.

Melt the white chocolate in a heatproof bowl over a pan of gently simmering water. Using a potato peeler, pare off curls from the dark chocolate.

Drizzle a little white chocolate over each cookie and scatter with some hazelnuts, rose petals, and dark chocolate curls. Let stand in a cool place to set for about 1 hour before using. They will keep, in an airtight container in a cool place, for a few days.

For vanilla ring cookies, make the cookies as above but omit the unsweetened cocoa and add an extra ¼ cup flour. To decorate, drizzle the cookies with melted dark chocolate and scatter with hazelnuts, candied rose petals, and white chocolate curls.

thumbprint cookies

Makes **14**
Preparation time **20 minutes**
Cooking time **20 minutes**

8 tablespoons (1 stick)
  unsalted butter, softened
¼ cup **packed light brown
  sugar**
1 **egg**, separated
½ teaspoon **ground mixed
  spice**
¾ cup **all-purpose flour**
¾ cup **almonds**, crushed
⅓ cup **strawberry** or
  raspberry jam
confectioners' sugar, for
  dusting (optional)

Beat the butter and brown sugar until creamy. Add the egg yolk, ground allspice, and flour and mix to form a soft dough. Lightly beat the egg white to break it up and turn it onto a plate. Scatter the almonds on a separate plate.

Shape the dough into small balls, 1¼ inches in diameter, and roll them first in the egg white and then in the almonds until well coated.

Place the balls on a greased baking sheet, spaced slightly apart, and flatten slightly. Bake in a preheated oven at 350°F for 10 minutes, then remove from the oven. Allow to cool a little, then lightly flour your thumb and make a thumbprint in the center of each cookie. Spoon a little jam into each cavity and return the cookies to the oven for an extra 10 minutes or until pale golden. Transfer to a wire rack to cool.

Dust the edges of the cookies with confectioners' sugar, if liked. They will keep, in an airtight container in a cool place, for a few days.

For peanut butter thumbprint cookies, make the cookies as above, using ½ cup crushed unsalted peanuts instead of the almonds. Fill the thumbprint cavities with smooth peanut butter instead of the jam.

traditional shortbread

Makes **8 pieces**
Preparation time **15 minutes**,
  plus chilling
Cooking time **45–60 minutes**

2 cups **all-purpose flour**
¾ cup **rice flour** or **ground
  rice**
⅔ cup **superfine sugar**, plus
  extra for dusting
pinch of **salt**
1 cup (2 stick) **unsalted
  butter**, softened

Sift the 2 flours (or flour and rice), sugar, and salt into a mixing bowl. Rub in the butter with your fingertips. When the mixture starts to bind, gather it with one hand into a ball. Knead it on a lightly floured surface to a soft, smooth, pliable dough.

Put the dough in an 8 inch flan ring set on a greased baking sheet. Press it out with your knuckles to fit the ring. Mark the shortbread into 8 pieces using the back of a knife. Prick right through to the baking sheet with a fork in a neat pattern. Cover and chill for at least 1 hour before baking, to firm it up.

Bake in a preheated oven at 300°F for 45–60 minutes, or until the shortbread is a pale cookie color but still soft. Remove the shortbread from the oven and let cool and shrink before removing the ring, then dust lightly with superfine sugar. When cold, cut into 8 pieces. It will keep, in an airtight container in a cool place, for a few days.

For cinnamon shortbread, sift 1¼ cups all-purpose flour, a pinch of salt, 1 teaspoon ground cinnamon and 2 tablespoons ground rice into a bowl and stir in ¼ cup superfine sugar. Rub in 8 tablespoons (1 stick) unsalted butter, then knead, shape, prick with a fork, and chill as above. Bake in a preheated oven at 325°F for about 40 minutes or until pale golden. Let stand on the baking sheet for 10 minutes, then cool on a wire rack.

linzertorte cookies

Makes **12**
Preparation time **30 minutes**,
 plus cooling
Cooking time **17 minutes**

8 tablespoons (1 stick)
 unsalted butter
⅔ cup **superfine sugar**
1 tablespoon **light corn syrup**
¾ cup **rolled oats**
1 cup **self-rising flour**
½ teaspoon **baking soda**
4 tablespoons **raspberry jam**
9 oz **white marzipan**
confectioners' sugar, for
 dusting

Heat the butter, sugar, and syrup gently until the butter has melted. Remove from the heat and mix in the oats, flour, and baking soda. Turn into a bowl and let stand until cool enough to handle.

Shape the mixture into 12 balls. Space them well apart on a greased baking sheet and flatten each slightly. Bake in a preheated oven at 350°F for 15 minutes.

Spread a teaspoonful of jam over the center of each cookie. Thinly roll out the marzipan on a surface lightly dusted with confectioners' sugar and cut out 12 rounds, using a 3½ inch round cookie cutter. Use a 2 inch round cutter to cut out the center of each round. Reroll the trimmings and cut into ¼ x 2 inch strips. Arrange 4 strips over each cookie to make a diamond pattern and place a ring of marzipan over the top. Cook under a preheated broiler for about 2 minutes until golden, watching closely because the marzipan will brown very quickly.

Transfer to a wire rack to cool and dust the edges of the cookies with confectioners' sugar. They will keep, in an airtight container in a cool place, for a few days.

For festive cookies, make the dough and shape into 12 balls as above. Flatten each to about 3¼ inches in diameter and space on a greased baking sheet. Arrange ⅓ cup small dried fruits around the edge of each cookie, then top with 4 chopped candied cherries, 1 tablespoon pumpkin seeds, and 2 tablespoons slivered almonds. Bake as above, omitting the jam and marzipan stage.

leftover turkey ideas

turkey & chestnut soup

Serves **6**
Preparation time **20 minutes**
Cooking time **3½ hours**

1 **turkey carcass**
leftover stuffing (optional)
2 **onions**, finely chopped
2 **carrots**, finely chopped
2 **celery ribs**, finely chopped
7½ cups **water**
cooked turkey, cut into bite-
   size pieces
2 tablespoons **oil**
2 large **potatoes**, diced
15 oz can **whole chestnuts
   in brine**, drained
3 tablespoons **sherry** or **port**
salt and **black pepper**

Break the turkey carcass into pieces and place in a large saucepan with the stuffing, if using, and 1 onion, 1 carrot, 1 celery rib and the seasoning. Add the measured water and bring to a boil. Cover and simmer for 3 hours. Add extra water as necessary.

Remove the carcass and vegetables and discard. Strain the stock and add the turkey meat.

Heat the oil in the rinsed-out pan, then add the potatoes and the remaining onion, carrot, and celery. Cook gently, stirring, for 5 minutes.

Pour in the turkey stock and bring to a boil. Simmer for 20 minutes, then add the chestnuts and sherry or port. Reheat and check the seasoning before serving.

For turkey & corn soup, omit the chestnuts and instead add a drained 11 oz can of corn kernels at the end of the cooking time. Warm through, season to taste, and serve the soup garnished with 1 tablespoon chopped parsley.

rigatoni with turkey & pesto

Serves **3–4**
Preparation time **5 minutes**
Cooking time **10–15 minutes**

8 oz **rigatoni**
½ teaspoon **salt**
2 tablespoons **extra virgin
   olive oil**
2¼ cups diagonally, thinly
   sliced **cooked turkey**
3 tablespoons **green pesto**
¼–½ cup **heavy cream**
salt and **black pepper**

To garnish
freshly grated **Parmesan
   cheese**
basil leaves

Cook the pasta in a large saucepan of boiling water
with the salt and 1 tablespoon of the oil for about
10 minutes, or according to the package instructions,
until al dente.

Heat a wok or large deep skillet over a moderate
heat until hot, then add 1 tablespoon oil and heat until
hot but not smoking. Add the turkey and stir-fry for
1–2 minutes.

Add the pesto and continue to stir-fry for 2–3 minutes,
until the turkey is heated through.

Drain the pasta well, add to the turkey mixture, and
toss over a high heat until evenly mixed with the turkey
and pesto. Add the cream, season to taste, and stir well
to mix. Serve garnished with Parmesan and basil.

For penne with turkey & red pesto, replace the
rigatoni with 8 oz penne and replace the green pesto
with 3 tablespoons red pesto. Add ½ cup pitted black
olives to the turkey and pasta mixture and heat
through before serving.

turkey & green bell pepper stir-fry

Serves **4**
Preparation time **15 minutes**
Cooking time **10–15 minutes**

3 tablespoons **canola oil**
⅓ cup **pine nuts**
1 **onion**, thinly sliced
1 inch piece of **fresh ginger**,
  very thinly sliced
2 **green bell peppers**, cored,
  seeded, and cut lengthwise
  into thin strips
3½ cups diagonally, thinly
  sliced **cooked turkey**
salt and **black pepper**

Sauce

2 teaspoons **cornstarch**
2 tablespoons **water**
2 tablespoons **soy sauce**
2 tablespoons **rice wine**
  or **dry sherry**
1 tablespoon **wine vinegar**
1 **garlic clove**, crushed
1 teaspoon **dark brown sugar**

Blend the cornstarch and measured water, add the remaining sauce ingredients, and set aside.

Heat 1 tablespoon of the oil in a wok, add the pine nuts, and toss for 1–2 minutes until golden brown. Remove and drain on paper towels.

Stir-fry the onion, ginger, and green bell peppers gently in the remaining oil for 3–4 minutes until softened but not coloured. Remove and set aside.

Stir-fry the turkey for 1–2 minutes, until heated through.

Whisk the sauce, add to the wok and bring to the boil, stirring until thickened. Add the pepper mixture and stir well to mix, then stir in the pine nuts. Season to taste and serve with rice or noodles.

For turkey & snow peas stir-fry, heat 2 tablespoons oil and stir-fry a grated 1 inch piece of fresh ginger and 2 sliced garlic cloves for 2 minutes. Add 1 roughly chopped onion and 2 cups snow peas and stir-fry for 3 minutes. Add 3½ cups cooked turkey, cut into thin strips, 3–4 scallions, cut into 1 inch lengths, and 3 tablespoons oyster sauce. Season lightly and stir-fry for 1–2 minutes, until the turkey is heated through.

turkey tetrazzini

Serves **4**
Preparation time **10 minutes**
Cooking time **15 minutes**

8 oz **spaghetti**
½ teaspoon **salt**
1 tablespoon **extra virgin olive oil**
3 tablespoons **butter**
⅓ cup **all-purpose flour**
2½ cups **turkey** or **chicken stock**
½ cup **heavy cream**
good pinch of **mustard powder**
2½ cups thinly sliced **cooked turkey**
3 tablespoons freshly grated **Parmesan cheese**
salt and **black pepper**

Cook the spaghetti in a large saucepan of boiling water with the salt and oil for 8–10 minutes, or according to the package instructions, until al dente.

Melt the butter in a saucepan, sprinkle in the flour, and cook over moderate heat, stirring, for 1–2 minutes. Gradually pour in the stock, beating vigorously after each addition. Bring to a boil, stirring, then reduce the heat and simmer, stirring, for about 5 minutes, until thick and smooth.

Remove from the heat, stir in the cream and mustard, and season to taste. Gently fold in the turkey strips.

Drain the spaghetti and spread half in the bottom of a lightly greased ovenproof dish. Cover with half the turkey mixture, then the remaining spaghetti. Top with the remaining turkey and sprinkle with the Parmesan.

Place in a preheated oven at 400°F for 10 minutes or until golden.

For turkey pasticciata, use 6 oz penne. Make a white sauce as above with 2 tablespoons each butter and flour and 2½ cups milk. Remove from the heat, add 1 cup diced mozzarella, 3 tablespoons grated Parmesan, a pinch of nutmeg, salt, and black pepper. Mix the pasta with 1¾ cups cooked turkey strips and add two-thirds of the cheese sauce. Pour into a baking dish. Mix 2 beaten eggs into the remaining sauce and pour over the top. Sprinkle with 3 tablespoons grated Parmesan and bake in a preheated oven at 375°F for 20 minutes.

turkey & lentil salad

Serves **4**

Preparation time **10 minutes**, plus cooling

Cooking time **45 minutes**

1⅓ cups **French green lentils** or **other lentils**

2 tablespoons **extra virgin olive oil**, plus extra to drizzle

1 **onion**, finely chopped

2 **red bell peppers**, cored, deseeded and finely sliced

2 **garlic cloves**, crushed

1 teaspoon **cumin seeds**

4 cups sliced **cremini mushrooms**, sliced

zest and juice of 1 **lemon**

handful of **flat leaf parsley**

1¾ cups sliced **cooked turkey**,

salt and **black pepper**

Cook the lentils in a large saucepan of salted boiling water for 35–40 minutes, or according to the packet instructions, until cooked al dente. Drain and transfer to a large salad bowl.

Heat the olive oil in a skillet and add the onion and red bell pepper. Cook over a medium heat for 15 minutes until beginning to soften, then add the garlic and cumin seeds and cook for 1 minute. Add the mushrooms, season with salt and black pepper, and cook for 2–3 minutes until they are softened.

Add the cooked vegetables to the warm lentils, stir in the lemon zest and juice and the parsley, and drizzle well with the oil. Season to taste. Let the salad cool to room temperature, then add the leftover turkey. Let stand to marinate for at least 30 minutes before eating.

For turkey & penne salad, omit the lentils and instead cook 10 oz penne in salted boiling water until al dente. Drain, refresh under cold running water, and drain again. Prepare the vegetables as above, then stir into the pasta with 1¾ cups cooked turkey, the lemon zest and juice, and the parsley. Instead of drizzling with olive oil, stir in ⅓ cup crème fraîche (or 2½ tablespoons sour cream mixed with 2½ tablespoons whipping cream) before serving.

turkey & almonds gratin

Serves **4**

Preparation time **15 minutes**

Cooking time **40–50 minutes**

3½ cups chopped **cooked turkey**

2 tablespoons **butter**

1 cup **blanched almonds**

½ cup grated **Parmesan cheese**

¼ cup chopped **parsley**

1⅔ cups **fresh whole-wheat bread crumbs**

Cheese & spinach sauce

2 tablespoons **unsalted butter**

¼ cup **all-purpose flour**

2½ cups **milk**

½ cup grated **Cheddar cheese**

1 **garlic clove**, crushed

3 cups **baby spinach**

salt and **black pepper**

Arrange the turkey in a shallow ovenproof dish. Melt the butter in a saucepan, add the almonds, and toss until they are golden. Sprinkle the nuts and butter over the turkey.

Melt the butter for the sauce in a saucepan. Sprinkle in the flour and cook, stirring, for 1–2 minutes. Add the milk, a little at a time, stirring after each addition, then simmer for 2 minutes. Add the cheddar and garlic, season to taste, and stir until the cheese has melted, then stir in the baby spinach.

Pour the sauce over the turkey, then mix together the Parmesan, parsley, and bread crumbs and sprinkle the mixture evenly over the turkey. Bake in a preheated oven at 325°F for 30–40 minutes until golden and bubbling.

For turkey, blue cheese & pine nuts gratin,

substitute 1 cup pine nuts for the blanched almonds. Omit the butter and toast the pine nuts under a preheated hot broiler for a few minutes, shaking to prevent burning. Set aside 3 tablespoons toasted nuts and mix the rest with the turkey in an ovenproof dish. Make a cheese sauce as above, replacing the cheddar with ½ cup crumbled mild blue cheese. Assemble the dish and bake as above, sprinkling with the reserved toasted pine nuts to serve.

turkey curry

Serves **4**
Preparation time **10 minutes**
Cooking time **25 minutes**

¾ cup **vegetable oil**
1 **onion**, sliced
1 inch piece of **fresh ginger**, finely chopped
2 **garlic cloves**, crushed
1 **red chile**, cut into rounds
1 teaspoon **ground coriander**
1 teaspoon **ground cumin**
¼ teaspoon **ground turmeric**
½ cup **water**
6 **tomatoes**, chopped
3½ cups cubed **cooked turkey**
2 tablespoons **plain yogurt**
juice of **1 lime**, plus extra wedges to serve
handful of **cilantro leaves**
salt and **black pepper**

Heat the oil in a large saucepan or wok and fry the onion for 8–10 minutes over a low heat, until it is soft and golden.

Add the ginger, garlic, chile and spices to the pan and stir-fry for 1 minute. Pour in the measured water and the tomatoes, bring to a boil, reduce the heat a little and simmer for 5 minutes. Season with salt and black pepper to taste, then stir in the turkey cubes.

Cover and simmer gently for 10 minutes, until piping hot. Remove from the heat, then stir in the yogurt, lime juice, and cilantro leaves. Serve with extra lime wedges and naan, if liked.

For turkey & spinach curry, follow the recipe above but omit the cilantro leaves and instead stir 3 cups baby spinach into the tomato sauce when adding the turkey. Complete the recipe as above, with yogurt and lime juice.

turkey waldorf

Serves **4**
Preparation time **20 minutes**

½ cup **mayonnaise**
2 tablespoons **lemon juice**,
   plus extra to taste
2⅔ cups shredded **cooked
   turkey**
3 **celery ribs**, sliced thinly
⅔ cup roughly chopped
   shelled walnuts
⅓ cup **raisins**
1 small **romaine lettuce**,
   thickly shredded
2 **Red Delicious apples**
salt and **black pepper**

Put the mayonnaise in a large bowl, add the lemon juice, and stir well to mix. Add the turkey, celery, walnuts, raisins, and lettuce leaves to the mayonnaise and mix well again.

Core and thinly slice the apples, then add immediately to the salad and stir well to coat. Season to taste and add more lemon juice, if liked.

For turkey curry mayonnaise, combine 3½ cups diced cooked turkey, 1 red apple, cut into small dice, 3 tablespoons golden raisins or raisins, 2 tablespoons roasted salted peanuts, ⅓ cup mayonnaise, 1 teaspoon curry powder, ½ teaspoon mild chili powder, and 1 tablespoon lime or lemon juice. Mix thoroughly and season to taste. Serve the mayonnaise on a bed of crisp lettuce leaves, garnished with cilantro leaves.

country turkey pie

Serves **6**

Preparation time **20 minutes**

Cooking time **35 minutes**

4 tablespoons **butter**

⅓ cup **all-purpose flour**

3 cups **milk**

1½ **chicken stock cubes**, crumbled

½ teaspoon **Worcestershire sauce**

1½ tablespoons **dry sherry**

3 drops **Tabasco sauce**

2⅔ cups diced **cooked turkey**

2½ cups sliced **mushrooms**

3 medium **carrots**, cooked and sliced

8 pearl **onions**, boiled

2 tablespoons chopped **parsley**

10 oz **store-bought puff pastry**, defrosted if frozen

a little **flour**, for dusting

beaten **egg**, to glaze

salt

Melt the butter in a large saucepan, sprinkle in the flour, and cook for 1 minute. Add the milk, a little at a time, stirring after each addition, then add the stock cubes and Worcestershire sauce and season with salt. Bring to a boil, stirring with a wooden spoon until the mixture thickens. Stir in the sherry and Tabasco sauce. Add the turkey, mushrooms, carrots, and onions and heat through gently but thoroughly. Stir through the chopped parsley, then turn the mixture into a 1¾ quart pie plate.

Roll out the pastry on a lightly floured surface and cover the plate, fluting the pastry edges. Make a small hole in the center to let the steam escape. Decorate with the trimmings. Bake in a preheated oven at 400°F for about 20 minutes, until the pastry is beginning to brown.

Brush the pie top with beaten egg, then return to the oven for an additional 10 minutes, until the pastry is puffed up and brown.

For turkey, ham & almond pie, brown 3 tablespoons almonds in 3 tablespoons butter. Stir in ¼ cup all-purpose flour, remove from the heat, and stir until blended. Add 1¼ cups dry white wine and 2½ cups chicken stock, bring to a boil, reduce the heat, and simmer for 1–2 minutes. Season well, then stir in ½ teaspoon dried marjoram and 2 tablespoons sour cream. Turn into 1¾ quart pie plate. Mix in 2⅔ cups diced cooked turkey, 4 oz diced ham, and ¾ cup halved seedless grapes. Cover and bake as above.

turkey sandwich

Serves **4**
Preparation time **10 minutes**
Cooking time **5 minutes**

8 **fatty bacon slices**
8 slices of **whole-wheat bread**
good-quality mayonnaise, for spreading
2 ripe **tomatoes**, sliced
small bunch of **watercress**
1 small ripe **avocado**, sliced
8 slices of **cooked turkey breast**
salt and **black pepper**

Broil the bacon for 3–4 minutes on each side, until golden and crisp. At the same time, toast the bread.

Spread 4 toast slices thickly with mayonnaise. Layer the tomatoes and watercress on top and add the avocado and turkey. Season well with salt and black pepper and top with the crispy bacon. Cover with the remaining toast and press down lightly. Serve at once.

For turkey wraps, replace the bread with 8 tortillas and the watercress with 2 little Boston lettuces. Chop the crispy bacon, finely chop the tomatoes, and shred the lettuce. Mix together with 2 tablespoons soured cream, a splash of Tabasco sauce, and a pinch of salt. Mash the avocado with the juice of 1 lime. Warm the tortillas under the broiler or in the oven, then spread with the mashed avocado, a spoonful of the bacon mixture, and a slice of turkey. Roll tightly and serve at once.

index